TEN SPIRITUAL LESSONS

I LEARNED AT THE MALL

other works by James F. Twyman

published by Findhorn Press

The Secret of the Beloved Disciple

Portrait of the Master

Praying Peace

The Praying Peace Cards *(October 2001)*

published by Warner Books

Emissary of Light

TEN SPIRITUAL LESSONS

I LEARNED AT THE MALL

James F. Twyman

FINDHORN
Press

First published by Findhorn Press in 2001

ISBN 1 899171 83 5

British Library Cataloguing-in-Publication Data.
A catalogue record for this book is available from the British Library.

Library of Congress Catalog Card Number: 00-109624

Edited by Tony Mitton
Layout by Pam Bochel
Front cover design by Dale Vermeer

Printed and bound in Canada

Published by
Findhorn Press

The Park, Findhorn
Forres IV36 3TY
Scotland
Tel 01309 690582
Fax 01309 690036

P.O. Box 13939
Tallahassee
Florida 32317-3939, USA
Tel 850 893 2920
Fax 850 893 3442

e-mail info@findhornpress.com
findhornpress.com

Contents

Introduction   7

Lesson 1   You Were Born Ready   17

Lesson 2   We Are All The Same   41

Lesson 3   Nothing Really Matters... Anyone Can See   55

Lesson 4   The Art of Divine Selfishness   71

Lesson 5   The Practice of What is True   79

Lesson 6   God Doesn't Care What You Do...
(but rather, who you are)   87

Lesson 7   The Declaration of Dependence   97

Lesson 8   Change is Not Necessary   105

Lesson 9   God is Rather Ordinary   113

Lesson 10   Love Conquers All   119

Acknowledgments   126

Introduction

BEGINNING THE RETREAT

Today I embark upon a journey unlike any I have taken before. It would be fair to say that I am somewhat experienced in spiritual matters, but this day marks a new chapter in my life, a daring departure from the adventures of my youth. It is only now, after long years of deep meditation, traveling to meet honored sages from distant lands, and after sharing my insights with thousands of thirsty aspirants, only now am I ready to enter this strange labyrinth. To have sought such high lessons before this may have led to my demise, for only now I am ready to sidestep the possible snares and temptations I am sure to encounter. Were I to have begun such a journey in my youth, there is no telling where it might have ended or what my fate would be. I am ready now, and so I step forward to begin my retreat, opening the door that leads to the hallowed hallways where my journey begins and ends — the mall.

How did I end up here to begin with? Oakville Place, forty minutes outside of Toronto, seems a strange place to begin this odyssey. I am better known for my foreign travels to countries like Bosnia, Iraq, Kosovo and Northern Ireland where I have promoted peace and sharpened my own spiritual methods and insights. I have written books on these great adventures, lectured around the world, and have performed my concerts in cathedrals and national theaters. I cannot decide if this new phase, the one that begins today, is a step forward or a step back. After all, I despise the mall... always have. I have gone to great lengths trying to avoid these walls and to dodge the effects of its seductive vapor. But also, it seems that I am no different than those who have gone before me, all the millions of shoppers who grace the corridors of malls such as this around the world. And it is precisely for this reason that I have decided to stay, for in the end this is how we prove ourselves. I must be willing, I have decided, to dive into the place where my resistance is highest, for it is here, on the branch furthest from the trunk of the tree, that the greatest lessons lie.

Many years ago I heard this call. When I was eighteen, a month after I had graduated from high school, I determined to leave the world of common desires and enter a monastery. I had been raised according to a strict Irish code that decreed a single recourse for a child bent upon the spiritual realms I enjoyed — priesthood. To this day, my mother regrets the day that, a year and a half later, I left those sacred corridors, as if she had somehow failed her son, her family, and God. After all, a mother such as mine measures her worth by a standard that may seem strange and foreign to most... for in the end only one thing matters — giving at least one son to the church. And yet the day I became a candidate in the order of Friars Minor is still etched in a favorable manner upon my brain. I remember opening those massive doors and being greeted by the other brothers. I remember rising early and joining the community for morning prayers and mass. And I recall how happy I felt to eat my meals in the penetrating silence of the monks' refectory, thinking that I had found my life, my purpose and the answers to every question I could ever have hoped to ask.

How could I have known how dramatically my life would twist and turn away from that time? And yet, there was one thing that never left me — the sense of the great value in leaving the mundane world and entering a spiritual retreat. The retreat may take place in the country, or in the desert, or in some hidden and secluded place, and it always follows a predictable rhythm of silence, reflection and sacred study. Whenever the harried pace of my life required such pause, I would begin the search, and each time it would end in a place very much like the monastery where I first began my quest.

Until now! The door I opened here at the mall could not be more different than those others. I stood and held the door open for two women pushing huge strollers, familiar patrons of this and every mall. Finally, when I too was within the bright, artificial environment with the muffled music and pretentious confidence, I knew that my spiritual journey had begun. As soon as I had conquered the beginning prejudice, I realized that this was the perfect place for me to begin this personal descent... or ascent, whichever.

A retreat such as this challenges the very foundation of one's life, and I realize that I have, until now, merely scratched the surface. After all, those other retreats were so easy for me. I have always thrived in the lighter air of spirit and soul, while all along it was here, in a shopping mall, that my greatest challenges lay. If I am to break free from the final chains that bind my life to mediocrity, then I must search out the environment where I am least at home. Then the shadows of my unconscious mind will rise before me that I may gain the power to vanquish what would have destroyed my soul. If I can but resist this tide as it sweeps across my life, then and only then will I be proven worthy. What greater, truer, more sacred place could I choose for this journey than what seems opposite in my mind — the mall.

"Yes," I said to myself, "this is what I have been waiting for. I pray now for the grace to spread my wings and fly through these artificially illumined corridors, to sink my roots deep into the ground in a place where no earth can be found. If I can make it through this, then anything is possible."

"Where are you calling from?" Karin asked.

"I'm at a mall outside Toronto," I said to her. "I hate malls, you know, and that's why I wanted to call. I have an idea I want to share with you. This place seems to have sparked something in me."

There was a long moment of silence on the other end of the phone, the sort of empty space that says more than words. If I could have crawled through the phone into my publisher's head, I'm sure I would have heard something like:

"Oh my God, here we go again. Two days from now the Spring Catalogue is due and now he wants to change everything... again. How am I going to get him to stick with one idea... to come up with a concept and stay with it? The other books weren't like this at all. He came in with a proposal and even made his deadline. This latest adventure seems to change daily. What is it now? The title? The subtitle? The whole book?"

"What's wrong with the direction you've been going?" she finally asked out loud. "I like everything you've written so far. Why not..."

"It just isn't working for me," I said. "It's boring, and I think I have writer's block. Every time I sit down to write I go blank. Then I came here and it all began flowing again."

"At the mall?"

"Yes, of all places… at the mall. I've been sitting here all morning looking around at the people and the stores. You know, I was wrong… the mall can be a very spiritual place. You just have to look at it in the right way.

"If you come in with the wrong attitude then all you see is the commercial crap and the people walking around as if they're asleep. Change the intent and everything else changes as well. It's like being on a retreat, like I'm back at the monastery or something. They're all angels in here teaching me about God, and truth, and enlightenment."

I stopped for a moment and listened to myself. I'm sure Karin thought I had gone off the deep end. Hours earlier I could have been seen pacing back and forth down the long corridor, from Sears at one end to The Bay at the other, lost in a daze of confusion. It all began as a sort of defense mechanism that helped me cope with the real reason why I was at the mall in the first place. A week earlier I had come here with my fiancée to search for an engagement ring. We had been making the jewelry store rounds for several days by then and by the time we arrived at Raffi Jewelers at the Oakville Place Mall I was nearly ready for a nervous breakdown.

As it turned out, Peter, the young manager at Raffi's, was the most helpful of the lot. I was impressed at how skillfully he attended to Siri Rishi, not too firm and without being a pushover. That would have been the kiss of death, for as confident as she seemed, the 'Love of my Life' required more than a little guidance. To leave her to her own devices, at least from my perspective, would have been disastrous. Peter and I seemed to be developing a powerful psychic connection, as if he could read my thought and knew exactly how far to let out the line before slowly, almost imperceptibly, reeling it back in again.

Before we left the store that day we were a single step away from a decision. Then, the following morning, we returned with confident smiles. Peter could see us from the rear of the store and came out to greet us.

"So, you're back," he said. "Does that mean the quest has ended? Are you ready to make a commitment?"

There was something about the way he said those words that knocked me off balance. I wasn't prepared to defend myself so early in the morning and had let my guard slip far too low. Siri Rishi, on the other hand, brightened her smile and squeezed my hand.

"Yes, I think he is," she said to him... or me... I'm not really sure which. "I mean, yes we're ready to put down a deposit."

It was a good save on her part and it seemed to take the heat off, if only for a moment. Wherever it was we were going, we would do it together, as a couple, as two people deeply in love. I smiled and let out a nervous sounding laugh. She looked at me out of the corner of her eye to make sure I was still with her, then stepped up to the counter.

Minutes later the deal was done. Siri Rishi described in detail how she wanted the ring to look, and Peter, just as he had the previous afternoon, responded with masterful skill. I just stood there watching, certainly overjoyed at the prospect, but another part of my brain was spinning out of control, lost in a sudden haze of strange confusion.

"How do you feel, honey?" she asked me.

"I feel fine," I said as I regained my composure. "I feel great."

"Are you sure you feel all right?" Karin finally asked, breaking the spell of my day dream.

"I feel fine. I feel great. What makes you say that?"

"Well, it's just that you can't seem to make up your mind what you're going to write about. This is at least the fourth idea you've had, and if we're going to get this into the Spring Catalogue we need something solid."

"The mall thing is good," I said with a little too much enthusiasm. "I mean, I think this could be a very good angle. When most people need a break or a spiritual retreat, they go to the mountains, or the desert, or to a monastery, to pray for a week. I've decided to spend a week at the mall and see what spiritual insights come to me. Think about it... it's so very original."

"Let me make sure I'm hearing this right. You want to spend a week in the mall? And how is this going to...?"

"Think about it this way," I said as I spun around, nearly wrapping the phone cord around my neck and strangling myself. "The masters have always said that enlightenment is not a change, but a recognition of what can never change. Do you see what I mean? Why not find enlightenment in a mall? It's filled with ordinary people, all of whom are fully enlightened without even realizing it. What if I spent a week talking to them, watching them? I should be able to experience enlightenment anywhere, not just beneath a Bodhi Tree. Maybe a mall would be more effective than an ashram because it's so real. I'm not running away from the world like you might think. I'm running toward it."

Once again... silence.

"Do you think I'm crazy?" I finally asked.

"I'm not sure," Karin said. "It's actually a wonderful idea... in a strange sort of way. But I have to ask you… are you under some stress? You seem different somehow, almost as if…"

"Grist for the mill," I said whimsically. "I wouldn't have come up with this idea if I was in a normal state of mind. I would just keep writing the boring book I started already. But this is so… it's so different… and wonderful. Why not take whatever neurosis I'm experiencing and make it work for me. Some of the greatest works of art have come from very difficult circumstances, you know."

"Okay, but you're all the way up in Toronto. What are you going to do if you end up chopping off your ear, or some crazy thing like that?"

"Karin, don't worry. I'm totally under control. Yes, this marriage thing has put me in 'shift mode' right now, but it's really a good thing. I'm happier than I've ever been before. It's just going to take me a little time to settle into the new rhythm. Writing this book will help."

"In a mall."

"Yes, in a mall. Why not? This is the modern equivalent of the Town Square, or Main Street in Middle America. This is where normal people go to shop and socialize… not people like you and me… well, you know what I mean."

"All right, go for it," she said. "But there's no going back this time. The catalogue goes to the printer in a week, and as far as I'm concerned you're writing a book about finding enlightenment in a mall. It does have an interesting ring to it."

"Now you're thinking like a publisher," I told her. "Leave it to me… it's going to be great… I hope. Either that or you may want to reserve a room for me at a mental hospital somewhere."

I hung up the phone and took a look around me. A woman

with an enormous stroller nearly wounded me, two thirteen year old boys gave me a passing look of contempt, and I saw a man standing nearby trying to console his two year old son who had just dropped his ice cream cone.

"Let the retreat begin," I said out loud.

Lesson 1

You Were Born Ready

"Peter, how are things?"

He stood behind the counter in the very place I saw him last, directly behind the engagement rings, all those sparkling diamonds that seem to speak a language all their own.

"Things are great. How are you… Jimmy, is that right?"

"Good memory," I said to him. "But it's the least I expect from the man I just gave… how much did that ring cost again?"

"Cost is relative," he said. "But satisfaction lasts forever."

Wow! What a great comeback. I was really starting to like this guy, not just in the ordinary "honest merchant/satisfied customer" sort of way, but as someone who might be able to assist me in my 'mall based retreat.' If I was going to spend the next five days there, it made sense to find a few allies... compatriots to soothe my wounded spirit, if it should ever become wounded.

"Yeah, I guess you're right," I said to him as I walked over to where he stood. "Satisfaction... right."

"Is there anything wrong?" he asked.

"No, not at all. I feel fine. I feel great." It was the third time I had said those words in the last two days. "It's just that... well, you've probably seen it a hundred times before. I'm not at all worried about getting married. Siri Rishi is wonderful. She's the best thing that ever happened to me. But, you know, there's a difference between saying something to someone, and having it become concrete. I asked her to marry me, and she said yes. So far so good, right? Then we came in here to buy the ring. You, being the wonderful jeweler you are, attended to us professionally and helped guide us toward the perfect choice. I then gave you my credit card. You ran it through your little machine over there and I signed the receipt. Very real. Do you see what I mean? I'm not backpedaling at all. I'm just trying to adjust to reality."

"You're right," he said in the most soothing tone possible. "I've seen it a hundred times before. There's nothing unusual about what you're feeling. In fact, you're about three steps ahead of most men. At least you're aware of what's happening. Most men would deny what they're feeling, lock it away somewhere and let it eat them alive. It's best to get it out, especially if you're capable of dealing with it, which you certainly are."

I felt like I had stepped into the office of my spiritual director, the first stop for anyone beginning a retreat. This is the person who is available to help navigate the tricky spots one normally encounters during such a sojourn. A spiritual director needs to be as solid as a rock, as wise as an old owl, and as relentless as a Minnesota winter. Not everyone is capable of the fine balance this requires. On one hand the retreatant needs to feel the sympathetic favor of their director, but the guide must also know when to push their charge a little harder than usual, past the snares and thorns that could wound their spirit. A powerful bond of trust must develop easily between the two, otherwise the retreatant will not feel the psychic safety net, a quality as necessary as a warm bed and a hot breakfast. Peter would be my spiritual director, and he didn't need to know anything about it.

"Thanks for the reassurance," I said to him. "I'm fine, really. Every once in a while I need to take a deep breath, and maybe even put my head between my legs. No, I'm just kidding. You've met Siri Rishi. She's wonderful, and I'm very lucky she chose me."

"You are… and I can tell she loves you very much."

"You think so? Yeah, of course she does. That's what makes it so easy… so comfortable. So, how's the ring coming along?"

"It's coming along just fine. It should be ready in about five days."

"That's perfect," I said to him. "The same day I'll be ending my… I mean, that works fine."

"You're going to love this ring. As I said before, it's not about the money, but the love you feel when you give it to her. Come here, I want to show you something."

We walked over to a showcase beneath a very bright spotlight. Peter put a key in the lock and leaned over to open a hidden drawer. The light caught his young face and made him look like an angel… until I rubbed my eyes and forced the vision away. Then he took something out of the drawer and held it out for me to see.

"Look at this diamond," he said. "This will be the center diamond for a ring a woman ordered a few days ago. Do you want to know how much that ring will cost?"

"How much?" I asked without taking a breath.

"Sixty thousand dollars. Quite a bit more than the ring you bought, right? So here's my question: Do you think that this woman will be twenty times happier than Siri Rishi? Not a chance...I guarantee it. You see, this woman is buying the ring for herself. It's not being given to her by a man who is deeply in love with her. And even if it was, just because it costs more doesn't mean it's more valuable. Maybe from an insurance point of view, but that's not what we're talking about, is it? When you give your ring to Siri Rishi, even though she picked it out herself, her face will be worth way more than sixty thousand dollars, because it's a smile you'll see in your mind for the rest of your life. Money can't buy a memory like that."

He opened the drawer and locked the ring back in the case. Then he stood up straight, put both hands on the glass counter and looked me in the eyes.

"There's nothing for you to be afraid of, you know. It's really a wonderful opportunity if you think about it. You're getting it all out of the way now so you don't have to deal with it later. Besides, the fear is already there… it just needs an escape hatch, a situation like this that will let you release it."

"The fear is already there," I repeated.

"Yes, the fear is already there. So don't worry about a thing."

"I won't," I said as I turned to leave. "Maybe I'll see you again, Father Confessor."

"You know where to find me."

The rumor was true. I was moving to Toronto. It was an obvious decision, really. Siri Rishi was a successful therapist and Drew, her 14-year-old son, had already started high school. The idea of all three of us moving to California was tempting, especially for Siri Rishi who hated the Canadian winter, but in the end we decided it would be best to let Drew finish school before moving south of the border. Luckily, my profession did not require that I live anywhere in particular. In fact, the idea of having a steady home was in itself a welcome change. There were certain legal issues that needed to be addressed, like permanent residency, but overall it was a non-issue.

As I sat in the food court at the mall that first day, I suddenly realized that the adjustment would be harder than I had first anticipated. It is a well-known fact among my friends that I am a coffee addict. As far as I'm concerned, this is not a cause for worry since I have long since given up all of the more destructive habits that could potentially cause greater harm. I accept what I have heard from my more health-conscious friends, that coffee disrupts this or that... but, in the end, a good cup of Joe makes me happy, and that seems to offset the potential ill effects.

I am also something of a coffee snob. If one were to do a general assessment of my personality, I'm sure they would find me to be the easy-going, compassionate sort who goes with the flow and rolls with the punches. This is true of nearly everything other than coffee. I have been known to voice my dissatisfaction in the event that a less-than-premium blend is passed off on me. It's one thing to stop at a gas station if you're driving cross country and there's no other choice. Such a decision is made to avert a caffeine emergency, not to satisfy a craving for "the good stuff." But if I'm in a café, the kind of place that sports a shiny copper cappuccino maker in full view, then I expect a cup at least five or six levels above the gas station brands. I've never thought this to be an unreasonable request.

Canada is a wonderful country and has more than its share of good coffee. Even Tim Horton's, the donut shop chain that never seems to be more than a stone's throw away from anything, brews an acceptable pot. If bad comes to worse, Tim Horton's is not a bad choice. But it is no substitute for Starbuck's, and the same goes for the other popular café chain, Second Cup. And here they were, directly in front of where I was sitting. They weren't more than fifty feet away from each other — Tim Horton's and Second Cup. It was going to be a tricky five days.

But I didn't want to be close-minded. I'm on retreat, I thought to myself, and being on retreat requires an open mind and a compassionate heart. It was best to approach the situation with a positive attitude and, who knows, maybe it would pay off in the end.

I walked over to the Second Cup and stood in front of the nervous man at the cash register. Looking at him I concluded that he managed the joint. He seemed to be in his middle to late fifties and bore an incredible likeness to William H. Macy, the bizarre car salesman in the movie Fargo. At first he didn't notice me standing there, so I cleared my throat to get his attention.

"Oh, I'm sorry," he said as he jumped backward.

"I didn't mean to startle you," I said. "I just wanted to..."

"Oh, no harm done, I was just daydreaming. Not a good thing to do at the register, I know. But now and then... I'm sorry, what can I get for you?"

"I'll have a large latte."

"A large latte," he repeated as he registered the request on the cash register. "Do you want 2% or skim milk?"

"Two percent, please."

"Great... two percent it is."

I paid him and he gave me my change. It was a small café and the only other employee, a young woman, seemed to be refilling the whole-bean canisters toward the back.

"Nice place," I said to him over the cappuccino maker.

"What was that?"

"Never mind," I said. "I'm not from Canada, so this place is new to me... the Second Cup, I mean. Hopefully it will..."

"I'm sorry, I can't hear you over the machine," he said, squinting his eyes as if that would help. He finished the latte and held it out to me. "Cocoa and cinnamon right there in front of you, and sugar's behind you on the shelf."

"Thanks," I said, as I walked over to the shelf and poured two sugars into the cup. Then I noticed that the cup that normally held the stirrers was empty.

"Do you have any of those little plastic sticks back there?" I asked. "Seems you're out over here."

"Oh, will you look at that," he said as if he had broken one of the most important rules he'd ever learned at the coffee academy. "It's hard to keep up on these things. It would be nice if other people noticed these things as well."

He raised his voice as he said those last words, turning his head in the direction of his young employee. She didn't seem to hear him.

"Nice place you've got here," I said again. He looked at me as if he thought I was mocking him, then relaxed his face and smiled.

"Well, thanks. Not much really, not with Tim Horton's down the way. They put out a good, cheap cup, so most people don't bother spending twice as much for a little flavor."

"Yeah, but you have the machine," I said.

"What do you mean?"

"The cappuccino machine… they don't have one."

"I'm waiting for the day when they get one… then I'm really in trouble."

The Coffee Man, as I began to think of him, turned and walked back behind the counter to take care of a new customer. I smiled as he left and sort of wondered what role he would play during my five-day retreat. I was sure it wasn't over, like someone you meet walking into a monastery at the same time, and you realize you're there for the same reason. He was on his own kind of retreat, I realized. We would see each other again very soon.

From an author's perspective, there are only a few feelings worse than walking up to a table in the center of a mall and seeing a stack of your own latest book beside a sign announcing, "All Books 90% Off." The sign really should read, "The publisher of this book was so pissed off it didn't become a best-seller that they unloaded 5,000 copies onto a remainder company for pennies apiece. Hope you enjoy it."

I held my breath as I walked from one table to another, praying not to see my name. This is, of course, the opposite of the prayer I normally say whenever I walk into Barnes & Noble, Borders, or the Canadian equivalent, Chapters. "Let it be face forward, Lord... Failing that, let it be on the end shelf... Failing that, let there be five or six copies available... and, Failing that, let them have one." Then I hold my breath, walk to the appropriate section and scan the shelf alphabetically, according to author's last name. "R... S... T... Twyman... one copy. All is not lost. They have one." If I'm really adventurous, I even offer to sign the copy... but normally I don't. One copy means it's not the pick of the month, which means they don't have the time or energy to waste on me. Move back into the shadows, Mr. Twyman.

But on this particular day I enjoy a kind of victory. There are no books bearing my name on the remainder table. Revitalized, I step away from the table of shame and find a seat in the food court. My coffee is still hot and it's a new day, I think to myself. Anything is possible, especially on the first day of a five-day retreat.

A few tables away I noticed The Coffee Man sitting alone, eating a sandwich. He looked so alone and tired, and a part of me wanted to reach out to him. After all, he was attentive to his customers and had a pleasant disposition, at least when he wasn't steaming milk. But there was something else I couldn't quite put my finger on, as if no one could touch him, even in this ocean of fluorescent light and nervous shoppers. Especially here. He didn't even look up from his food, but kept his eyes locked on the white bread and sliced ham. I had to say something to break through his despair. I thought about how lucky I was to have not imposed a silent retreat on myself.

"Hello Coffee Man," I said as I moved to the bench across from him. "I hope you don't mind if I call you that. I'm sorry, you probably don't remember me... I'm the guy who..."

"Sure... You're drinking my coffee... I remember you... large latte, 2% milk."

"That's right... You probably remember all of your customers... not by name, of course, but by the coffee they drink."

"I've been doing it awhile," he said, suddenly very happy to have someone to converse with. "I took over this café a couple of years ago, but before then I managed a café in Toronto... ten years I was there... little neighborhood place... the sort of café where you really get to know your customers. Here, well, it's just a mall. Different people every day."

"Just a mall," I parroted.

"Yeah, just a mall. People come and go... so I remember coffee, not names."

"I'm learning to look at the mall in a new way," I told him.

"What do you mean?"

"It's hard to explain, but... you see, I've always hated malls. Artificial social environments... that's the way I always looked at them. But today it's teaching me a new lesson. I can decide to see it in the way I always have, or I can change my mind and see it through the eyes of grace."

I was afraid I'd lost him, especially the line about grace. He looked at me with puzzled eyes, then began to wrap the remaining half of his sandwich into the wax paper.

"What do you mean?" he finally asked, pausing for another second before leaving me altogether.

"Well, I've always had this elitist attitude about malls... which really means that I'm making myself out to be better than the people who shop here. Right? Well that's nonsense. So I've decided to start afresh, as if I've never been here before, and realize I'm no different from any of these people... no different from you. We're all filled with grace, which just means that God loves us. I've decided to focus on that rather than the crap I've been seeing."

He relaxed and eased back into his seat. I had won him, if only for a moment.

"Are you a Christian?" he asked.

"Well, sure, why not? Yes."

My answer obviously confused him and I decided to offer more.

"Let me explain. I was raised Christian — in fact, I was once studying to be a priest. But now it's kind of like this mall. I used to focus on how I was different from everyone else. I had different beliefs than, say, a Buddhist. I used those differences as a way to separate us rather than bring us together. Now I choose to focus on the things in which we're the same. Take peace, for example. We all want to live lives of peace, whether we're a Christian, a Jew, a Hindu... whatever. So if we focus on that, then the differences just melt away."

"But what about Jesus?" he asked.

"What about him? He's the man for me... for sure. But it's more than that as well... It's about focusing on what Jesus taught, not his personality. He taught peace, right? He taught compassion, just like the Buddha or any other enlightened being."

The Coffee Man finished wrapping his sandwich and stood to leave.

"Are you going to be here tomorrow?" he asked.

"Why?"

"I have a few things you should read. It might turn you around, if you don't mind my saying."

"I don't mind at all, and I would love to read anything you bring for me."

"Great, I'll see you then. I'll even give you a free latte, on the house."

"That would be great," I said as he walked away. "I'll read anything if you keep my cup full."

As I sat facing the row of 'children's stationary vehicles,' I knew that they would become one of the mysteries I would need to solve during my retreat. It is normal for a spiritual director to offer a poem, or a book written by a great saint, for the retreatant to ponder during the span of their stay. Often the sacred passages stir a particular insight that sets the tone for the whole retreat, and it is only when the lesson is fully absorbed into the soul that one can say the retreat is complete. Otherwise it continues long after the retreatant has been dismissed, even years later when the details of the retreat are just a faint memory.

"What are these strange vehicles trying to teach me?" I asked myself.

There is the brightly colored ice-cream truck pulsing back and forth whenever a quarter is deposited into its slot. Moving left, we come to the tiny locomotive that slides forward and back on a section of metal track. Then there is the cartoonish horse, something I once saw in a nightmare. Finally, beside the horse, is the smiling cactus with the sombrero. As far as I could tell, the cactus doesn't move at all, just sits there and watches the others.

I sat and finished my coffee and watched as the parade of children desperately cajoled, or tried to cajole, quarters from their disheartened parents. But why were they disheartened? Was it the unconscious frustration one feels watching a child enjoy a ride that looks pretty but goes nowhere at all? Or is it the mall itself, the way the lights and the sounds and the cry of the children work upon the psyche? This would become one of the main questions of my retreat, I began to realize. Solve this mystery and the others would open like flowers before my eyes.

Some parents gladly offered the shiny coin that had the power to pacify their child for thirty seconds or so. But most found themselves engaged in a battle they would never win. A child spots the ice-cream truck from a distance and makes a beeline for its carriage as the parents scream for them to stop. By the time the parent catches up, the child is already within the grip of the toy, and prying them loose attracts more than a few stares. In the end the parent either gives in and coughs up the coin, or pulls the screaming child back to the stroller where they are strapped in, kicking and screaming.

Behind those seductive miniatures a golden sign is hanging on the wall. It reads: "Change is Available at the Concierge Desk." It is a kind of a clue, I decided. As far as I could tell, there were two possible explanations for this sign... one is quite obvious, and the other is metaphysical. I was willing to consider both, but I was starting to believe it was the latter.

There was only one way to find out. I was off to visit the concierge.

"Hello. I was hoping you could help me change."

The woman at the Concierge Desk looked confused and lost. "I'm sorry… I don't understand what you mean."

"I saw a sign by the… whatever you call those little vehicles over there that don't really go anywhere, that said, 'Change is Available at the Concierge Desk.' That's why I'm here… I need to change a few things about myself."

The woman glanced over at a portly, stern looking security guard who was already onto me. He took the cue and slid behind the desk.

"I think you misunderstood the sign," the woman said. "That's there in case a mother doesn't have change for the toys… she can come over here and we'll give it to her."

"Yes, I understand," I said as I leaned in closer. "But there's a change machine over there already, you know, the one that looks like a gasoline pump. Well, I started to think that maybe there was more to this change thing than was initially apparent."

"Sir, is there something I can help you with?" The security guard had decided it was time to step in, as though I were going to end up being a problem.

"No, there's no problem here, Officer… Maze, yes… great name. I was just wondering about the sign over by the…"

"Yes, I heard," he said directly. "As she explained, that's for parents who need change for the machines. Okay?"

"Yes, absolutely… I was just digging a little deeper I guess… looking for some hidden spiritual insight that isn't there at all. I apologize."

"No problem, sir. Enjoy the mall."

As I walked away, I could feel them both staring at me as if I was a potential problem. How could I explain what was really happening… that I had to test the boundaries to determine the most essential lessons? I looked back and smiled, a reassuring smile to make them feel at ease. The look on their faces didn't change at all.

I walked to the far end of the mall, all the way to The Bay, one of the two department stores that anchor Oakville Place. I was starting to feel a little embarrassed by my confrontation at the Concierge Desk, the result, I felt, of the strangeness of my situation and the nagging nervousness I still felt regarding the retreat's primary catalyst — "the engagement ring." I didn't want to be banned from the center on my first day, so I decided it was best to fix my attention upon a different area of the mall.

I sat down on the bench that was only a few feet from a fountain with a surprisingly artistic statue in the center. It was a true work of art, nothing like the tacky, commercial fare that decorates most malls. The abstract piece was of two women, joined at the base, each one holding a kind of shell and sharing the water that poured between them. The rusty green color of the fountain gave it an ancient look, as if it had been sitting in a garden gathering moss for a hundred years. It's hard to say why it comforted me the way it did. Perhaps just the fact that even here, in this commercial mecca, the place I had chosen for my strange retreat, one can find beauty and grace. It became the metaphor that I would fall back on again and again during the five days I had set aside.

I remembered the friary where I lived for a time so many years before, when I was a Franciscan. Whenever I had wondered why I was there, why I had chosen to walk a path that felt so out of place in my young life, I would sit outside in front of the secluded fountain with the statue of St. Francis in the center. He was the one who drew me there in the first place, the blessed patron of all things mystical. There was a look in his eyes that made me forget whatever trouble plagued me in that moment. He was in the world but not of the world. I was in the mall but not of the mall. What a strange position to find myself in. Maybe the women in the fountain would console me the way St. Francis used to. There was something about the shells that seemed to be calling to me, something about the gift of water. Another mystery, I thought to myself. Another intriguing mystery for my attention.

Above me, a speaker pumped out the never-ending ten-year-old pop music that sounded through the entire mall. I tried to focus on the sound of the water as it fell from the bronze ladies onto the ceramic tile. The two sounds competed for awhile before the music finally won the battle. I looked around at the dozen or so people who walked down the long corridor, darting in and out of the stores. I wondered if they even heard the music, or how many of them ever stopped to look at this wonderful fountain.

"I'm ready for this," I said just beneath my breath. "Whatever this means, I'm ready."

I didn't expect to see a shoe repair shop nestled between the fast-food stands in the food court. It didn't seem to belong there, or in any twenty-first century North American mall. Europe, perhaps, or at the end of some sweet little cobblestone street in New York or San Francisco, but not here. The bright lights of the mall were a glaring reminder of why I had chosen this place to dive into my soul, and the little shop repairing shoes in the corner was either there to mock or redeem me.

I hovered near the shop for fifteen minutes or so, hoping to unravel the mystery. When on a retreat it is important to look at everything with a penetrating gaze, for every item, every moment, has a lesson to teach; even in the mall, where I felt like a foreigner, especially in the mall. Heaven was waiting to open before me. The shoe repair shop proposed a certain challenge which I was all too happy to accept. We were very much the same, I thought to myself, displaced as I was in the land of consumer paradox where nothing is how it appears to be. Maybe that was the lesson I was to learn, for in the end this applies to us all, even shoe repair shops.

The shop itself was barely more than a large closet with its ancient looking, strange machines and shoe-soles hanging about as if they were trophies. Behind the counter an old Oriental man with a leather apron stood shining a pair of black Florsheims. Why did I expect something less strange? For by then the set-up was clear. This was the corner of the mall that time forgot, like a quantum vortex where the past and present converged creating a scene that was neither one nor the other.

I finally gathered enough courage to enter into the vortex. But what would happen to me if I wandered so close, if I dared challenge the boundary that separated the shopping mall from such awesome power? Would I evaporate, be transported to another city and find myself in an identical shop on the other side of the world? I playfully entertained all of these possibilities, while at the same time moving toward the shop in a manner that would not betray my better intentions.

The Oriental man didn't seem to notice me as I stood looking at the wide assortment of shoelaces that lined the wall. One or two older women had entered behind me, one to pick up a pair of shoes and the other to browse. I waited for them to leave, for me to be alone with the Shoe Man, before finally turning around to face him.

"Your shoes not ready yet," he said, barely looking up from his work.

"I'm sorry?"

"I said, your shoes not ready... need more time to finish. Come back in half hour. By then they will be ready."

Was it fate that he had mistaken me for someone else? This was the perfect opening, and from here I would advance into the unknown, and what would happen then only God knew.

"I'm sorry, but you must have me confused with someone else," I said. "I don't..."

"Oh, then, your shoes are ready," he said as he reached beneath the counter and placed a shoe box on top. "I mistook you for someone else. I'm very sorry, but here are your shoes. That will be ten dollars."

He looked at me and wondered why I wasn't reaching for my wallet.

"Once again, we seem to be confusing one another," I said to him. "I am not waiting for shoes... I haven't given you any to repair... at least not yet."

"Oh, once again, I am so sorry," he said as he placed the box beneath the counter again. "Then you have shoes to repair?"

"No, not exactly," I said. And with that we both stood confused, for I was so caught up in the moment that I hadn't planned what to say to him. He looked at me, then smiled as if he suddenly understood.

"Oh, I know why you are here," he said.

At first I didn't know how to respond. Was it true? Did he possess such insight? Maybe my fantasy of the shop caught between the two worlds was true, and he was, in fact, a Zen master who would guide me through the trials of my retreat. Why did I expect anything less? Had I not chosen this mystical path and wasn't it realistic to expect such miracles? I looked back at him and smiled.

"You really know why I'm here? For real?"

"Yes, I do," he said. "You want to apply for the job. I told you

I knew. Well, I am sorry but the opening doesn't come till next week, but you can fill out application form now. Then I will call you."

"Okay... why not." I didn't see the harm in filling out the application. It actually gave me a reason to linger for awhile, to search out the mystery this place obviously held. I stood to one side of the counter and gave the requested information, never once wondering what he would think when he read it. There was no indication, at least according to my past work history, that I was either qualified for, or interested in, such a job. I had to search back nearly eight years to the last time I even had a real job, working as an advertising sales rep for a newspaper in Madison, Wisconsin. I certainly wasn't going to refer to my recent work history, for that would really cause suspicion. In the end I decided to make it all up. After all, it was a ruse, a ploy to keep talking, and I wasn't at all interested in being a shoe repairman myself.

All the while the old Oriental man stood looking at me, smiling. In one hand he held a shoe that was already nicely shined, and the ancient cloth he held in the other was much like him — bright and worn. There was something about his eyes that made me feel at ease. If I were, in fact, looking for a job, I might very well have taken the application seriously.

"Are you ready?" he asked me.

"Am I ready... for what?"

"Are you ready for life?"

This was a very strange question indeed, given the circumstances, but it seemed to support my earlier theory. His eyes never dimmed when he asked me this, and his hands never lost their elegant rhythm, the dance he made between the shoe and the bright orange cloth.

"Yes, I am ready for life," I finally said. "Why do you ask?"

"Because working in a shoe repair shop is very much like life," he said to me. "People bring me their worn, dull shoes and expect me to bring them back to life, like a healer. Few people realize the importance of this, for our shoes are vastly underrated. Think about it — if your shoes hurt your feet, then they are worthless, no matter how well shined. But if they are comfortable you don't even think about them. You go through the day with a smile, though you don't know why you are so happy. Happy feet — happy life. This is my motto."

"Happy feet — happy life. That's great."

"Don't you agree? Is it true that your feet determine the direction not only of your step, but also of your mood?"

"Yes, to a certain extent. You asked me if I was ready... ready for life. So, for you, shoes are a metaphor for life. Is that correct?"

"Oh, more than a metaphor," he said as he suddenly burst out laughing. "More than a metaphor... I'm a poet and didn't know it."

I laughed as well, then put the completed application on the counter in front of him. Even if it wasn't funny, he was a good man and I didn't want to leave too fast.

"Yes, I am like a healer," he continued. "We are all healers, aren't we? What do you heal? Let me look at this paper and see."

He read the application as if he was reading my fortune. His tiny eyes squinted and he hummed a bit to himself, obviously reading more into what I wrote than was actually there.

"You heal by selling advertising?" he laughed. "Well, why not... even then you must talk to people and help them. Right? Are you now ready to heal people's feet as well as their souls... or shall I say soles?"

Once again he burst out laughing, overjoyed that he had stumbled across another pun.

"I am ready for... whatever," I said. "I was born ready."

"That's a very good attitude. You know, nothing can really

happen till we realize we are ready. Till then we walk around trying to get ready, and life just passes us by. I come from China, and I lived there till I was forty-five years old. I have been here now for twenty years, and in this mall for five. All my life I have fixed shoes, and I tell you that it is a very important job, though highly underestimated. I learned the old ways from my father, and he from his father. In China this was a very admirable profession, but here it is overlooked. Most people go and buy new shoes when the old ones wear out. Look at this pair I am shining now. There is still so much life left. All it needs is a little attention and love. Attention and love go so far, even now, even here in the mall."

I was right, he was a Zen master. Oh, how happy I was at that moment, for I knew I was not alone in my retreat. When in doubt I could always come back to the Shoe Man and he would show me the way. Who knows, maybe I'll end up like him, shining shoes and dispensing wisdom to unwary passersby.

"I know you don't have an opening now, but would you mind if I came back and talked more? I'm going to be hanging around the mall for a few days and would enjoy visiting with you."

"I am here, and I will remain here," he said, suddenly becoming serious. "Why do you think I have this job. I save soles, and souls. Come back whenever you want."

On the second floor of the Oakville Place Mall there is an upscale lingerie shop with beautiful bras, negligees and underwear displayed in the window. A dozen or so women shopped inside as I watched, scanning through the displays and samples, thinking thoughts that no man can ever understand. Men enjoy lingerie, even adore it, but none of them truly understand it. That is perhaps why it is so enticing. I sat down on a bench outside the shop and considered this mystery. Most men will agree that a woman in beautiful lingerie is far more exciting than a woman with nothing on at all. Why? Is it the fabric we are attracted to, or what lies beneath? Or is it that we are always drawn toward what is hidden from us? If this is true, there would probably be a mad dash toward Islamic countries where women show little more than their blinking eyes. I became convinced that if I were to solve this mystery, I would probably also discover some great spiritual truth.

I started to feel a little guilty about sitting there, staring at the shop window. Anyone who noticed would probably never realize that I was attempting to crack a deep spiritual mystery. More than likely I would be written off as a weirdo, and the security guard would soon be summoned, the very same guard I had had trouble with before. Seeing me leering by the lingerie shop would be all he needed to usher me to the door once and for all. Then where would I be? What an insult to be kicked off a retreat on the first day. What kind of an example would I be setting?

I shifted to the other side of the bench and tried to pretend that I was looking in the other direction. But no matter how hard I tried, my eyes, my body, my whole self seemed to rotate back to the shop with the bras, underwear and beautiful lingerie.

Perhaps I wasn't ready after all.

I walked back to the fountain where I could collect my thoughts. Three hours had already passed since I began my "mall retreat," and I was just as confused as I had been at the start. But why should I expect anything else?

It was like a spiritual detox, the natural release of all the vain tendencies so common to the ego. There was no reason to expect them to depart with ease, in only half a day, for they had never been "gracious guests" in the first place. The ego never dissolves... it leaves kicking and screaming, holding on to anything it can, gasping for breath. The trick is not to buy into the drama. Better to let it have its say, make whatever noise it wants, then send it on its way. It is, after all, rather hard to box with an opponent that never puts on gloves.

As I sat looking at the statue of the two women sharing water, I remembered what it was that sparked the retreat in the first place. The ring. I started to realize that the fear I felt was really the cause of a deeper fear — that I wasn't ready to get married. I was obviously not afraid of a small gold band with a few diamonds, but of what it represented. In this case, the ring represents commitment, stability and responsibility. I had spent most of my life pushing those things away, preferring in their stead a life of uncompromised freedom. I would be ready for those others later, in a few months, or a few years, but never now.

But the fact is that I was always ready, not only for commitment but for the deeper realities we run away from with equal speed and enthusiasm. Marriage itself is a symbol of the relationship we share with the Divine. As I watched the statue in front of me, with the water pouring from one woman to the other, I realized that this is how we finally tune ourselves to those deeper activities. Being ready to give ourselves to each other is the same as giving ourselves to God. They cannot be separated. I wasn't afraid of a ring, or marriage, or Siri Rishi. I was afraid of God. As soon as I realized that, it felt like the ice broke. You can't realize that there's nothing to be afraid of till you realize you're afraid. How simple. Then, and only then, are you ready to take the step away from fear and into the light. That is the only thing we're really here to do. Realizing that we're ready is only the first step.

I felt like I had achieved a kind of victory or breakthrough. A rush of energy filled my soul, and so I stood up from the bench and thanked the two cement ladies for the lesson they had helped me learn. A successful retreat is made up of a succession of lessons and insights that are learned, and then applied to one's life. One victory leads to another lesson, till they all string together like pearls creating a whole necklace. I had my first pearl, and I held it very tightly in my hand.

"I'm ready for this," I said out loud. "I'm ready for all of it, though I can't even see past where I now stand. But in spite of that, I keep moving."

I walked away from the fountain and began looking for the next adventure.

Lesson 2

We Are All The Same

I entered the record store as if it were a shrine. If I had not been paying close attention, if I had let my guard down and allowed myself to revert to the ingrained reverence I learned as a young Catholic boy, I might have even genuflected at the door. That's how much music means to me. It is more than the harmonies, or rhythms, or the plastic disks carrying digital codes that produce the most marvelous sounds when played. Music is like a sacrament, and it has the power to lift one's mood or one's hope, even the hope of a whole country or the whole world. When scientifically applied, music can help restore a person's health, both physically and mentally. But like any other force, it can also be used to imprison, delude and manipulate. History overflows with examples of both.

But this was a mall record store, more of a naive reflection of popular tastes than a tool for those who would oppress or liberate. This was not a place where philosophy ruled, but the billboard charts, or the current teenage sensation that would be forgotten in a week or two. Its power had been reduced to the point that it was hardly recognized, and those who entered this sacred place were like tourists that visit a Gothic cathedral to admire the architecture, not to pray. I, on the other hand, walk silently between the rows of disks lest I disturb these saints. Perhaps I am overly sentimental, but I am, after all, a musician myself, and it is only right that I put music upon so high a peak.

Why do I still refer to it as a record store? Gone are the days of leafing through stacks of large cardboard folders with vinyl disks the size of Frisbees. Technology has advanced since then and compact disks now rule the world. I doubt there is a mall in North America that has a "real" record store in it. One would have to leave the suburbs and enter the din of the city to find such an endangered species, far away from the bright fluorescence of Oakville Place. Once there, you would likely find a 30-something coolie with shoulder-length hair who is more a walking encyclopedia than a merchant. Ask any question you want about jazz, classic rock or punk and you're sure to get an intelligent answer. Ask for the latest pop release and you're likely to get thrown out the window.

"Excuse me, is there anything I can help you with?"

She had crept up behind me so quietly that I hadn't even noticed her. This was a wonderful beginning because it showed respect, not so much for me but for the hallowed ground we stood on. She was a young woman, maybe twenty, which surprised me a little. It is unrealistic to expect someone so fresh to be more than a novice, and I decided to press her a bit to see what she knew.

"I'm looking for a Miles Davis CD, sort of a late period release, something to do with Spanish... "

"You mean Sketches of Spain. God, I wish. You think you're going to find something that cool here? Not likely. Mention any rap CD and we've got three copies, or fifty, but real music, well, you'll be hard pressed."

"How about Richie Haven's..."

"How about I beat you senseless?"

"I guess that means no?"

"Right."

"You know a lot about music, don't you?"

"I'm the youngest girl, by far, in a family with five boys. They were raised with different values, the sort that hardly exist any more. But I was trained straight out of the womb. I was listening to early Who and Traffic when most of my friends were into Kids on the Block. God, I hated them."

"Yeah, I know what you mean."

"What are you doing here, anyway?" she asked.

"Why do you ask?"

"You don't seem like you belong, like you're not the same... well, you know what I mean. You're more like me, in taste anyway."

"Then what are you doing here?"

"Serving time. What else? Trying to save up enough money to get my own place in Toronto, or anywhere else. For now, I'm still at the rents."

"The rents?"

"You know — Parents."

"Oh, I get it."

"You're from the U.S., aren't you?"

"How can you tell?"

"I'm not sure. I just have a way of knowing these things. Maybe I'm psychic or something."

"What else do you know?"

"Let me think for a moment." She reached out and put her finger on my temple, a move which startled me. Then she closed her eyes and made like she was reading my mind. I wondered if she really was. "You're here looking for something, but it's not something you can find in a mall."

"What do you mean?"

"You tell me. Was I right?"

"That sort of depends. Yes, I'm looking for something, and at first I didn't think I would find it in a mall, but now I think I might."

"This has nothing to do with a CD, does it?"

"Not really," I said. "I'm just here wasting time. Thought I'd check out your stock. Not all that impressive, is it?"

"I already told you that."

"Then why do you work here?"

"I already told you that, too. Though it ain't much, it's the hippest place in the mall, and I'm the hippest chick, so you see, we go together."

"I can see that."

"No, I'm just kidding. Do you live here or are you just visiting?"

"May be moving here. I'm getting married to an Oakville native."

"Too bad."

"Why do you say that?"

"I'm trying to get out, and you're trying to get in."

"But we're in different life stages. I've been roaming all over the world for a long time. You're just getting ready…"

"I've been around a little, too… went to Europe last summer and toured around… you know, doing the youth hostel thing. It was really mad."

"Really mad… that's a very English sounding remark."

"Been there too."

I spent a few more moments going back and forth with my young music lover. It wasn't until I was halfway down the hall that I realized I didn't even ask her her name.

"Gives me a reason to go back," I said to myself.

Record stores are to Catholicism what bookstores are to Protestantism. Both supply an endless assortment of information, inspiration and perhaps even aggravation, depending upon what you're looking for at any given moment. But the one is ultimately linked with faith or the intellect, and the other with a deeper experience that mental concepts can never ascend to. Now here's the trick — which is which is purely a matter of opinion. I, for one, tend to rotate the two on a regular basis.

But on that particular day the Catholic Church was represented by all things musical, and the intellectual pursuits of the Protestant Reformation were represented by the book industry. After all, the glory of music lies in its ability to take one away from the mind into the heart where those deeper currents ride. One could compare this experience to the incense and rituals of a Catholic mass. Books, on the other hand, tend to rely upon well-developed arguments and provable facts more than upon the ethereal qualities music would inspire. There are exceptions, of course, on either side, but that's the beauty of religion. You can use it to prove almost any point you want to prove.

I remember attending a Unity Church in Chicago years ago, and the minister made a statement that has stuck with me ever since. He said that the difference between a person who is religious and a person who is spiritual is that the religious person believes in hell and the spiritual person has been there. This would probably qualify the majority of the population for the spiritual life rather than the religious.

"May I help you find a book?"

I thought about how different this woman was from my new friend at the record store. At first glance she was obviously from a whole different era. I picked her to be in her mid-fifties. Secondly, she lacked the natural charm that came so easily to the "hippest chick in the mall." This was her job, damn it, and she was serious about it. She stood behind the counter with a straight spine and a tight jaw. If I didn't really want to look around, I might have run away, never to return.

"Um, no. I'm just looking, thanks."

"I'm here."

"What was that?"

"I'm here… if you need me." Her eyes became like large beams when she said these last four words. I couldn't tell if she wanted to be needed or if it was a supreme inconvenience. She had staked out her territory behind the counter, hovering over the cash register, and I had the feeling that drawing her out would be like pulling her from her lair of safety. What else was there to do, then, but take her up on her offer.

"Actually, yes… I do need help. Do you have any books by

Rilke, the German poet?"

She pointed a straight finger toward the far corner of the store. "The poetry section is over there, "she said.

"Could you show me... I mean, I get so confused in stores like this... maybe you could help me find it."

It was like prying a bear's claws loose from its lunch. I could see the instant fear that overcame her, as if her worst nightmare was coming true. She had to leave the cash register and venture out into the shelves, and people, and God knows what else. Her eyes darted back and forth as if looking for another clerk that could bail her out. They must have been at lunch for no matter how hard she looked, there was no one else around.

"Yes," she finally said, "I can help you."

Her strategy was to walk as fast as she could, not even looking back to see if I was still with her, point out the requested shelf, then sprint back to the safety of the counter. I was right behind her, for I was intrigued by this game and didn't want to waste the opportunity to see it through to the end.

"Here we are, the poetry section. Now if there isn't anything else... "

"Actually, yes there is," I said, noticing that the cracks in her face had suddenly deepened. "I notice you have an anthology of Rilke's poetry, but I'm looking for my favorite... 'Letters to a Young Poet.' Do you know it? It's not really poetry but a collection of letters Rilke wrote to..."

"Yes, I know the book. It may be in the classic section. Please follow me."

I kept pace with the woman, hardly an easy task since she now seemed determined to finish with me, then resume her natural position behind the counter. We arrived at the proper shelf and scanned the titles. It wasn't there.

"Please follow me back to the counter and I'll be happy to order it for you."

She was practically half way back to the cash register when I stopped her again. "Before you go, one more question." She turned around slowly, like a gunslinger ready to mow me down. Then, with slow, deliberate steps she walked back to where I stood.

"Yes sir… what else can I do for you?"

"I was wondering if you have any books by James Twyman… maybe in the New Age section."

"Never heard of him."

"Well, I guess he's not the most well-known author you have, but he's done well, considering everything."

"Considering what?"

"Everything… you know."

"I'm not sure I'm following you, sir."

"Never mind. Could we check."

"I really don't think…"

"Yes, I know, but you never know… you might just be surprised."

By the time I finished this sentence she was already on her way to the New Age section. With lightning speed she scanned the shelf, then stopped toward the very bottom.

"Emissary of Light, one copy."

"One copy."

"Yes, would you like to buy it?"

"No, I was just wondering if you had it."

She was back at the counter before I knew it, and her claws were once again tight in the wood. I walked around for another minute or two, then decided to leave. I smiled at her as I passed but she looked the other way.

"Oh well," I thought to myself. "There's always the record store."

My mind was spinning out of control. How could the two places I honored most be so different in this mall? The encounters seemed to reflect my own confusion, the self-imposed seesaw between my career as a musician and my career as an author. Which was more dominant in my life, and was it bad manners to claim both?

I sat down on a bench to consider the evidence. On one hand, it was my music that had launched my career as an author, so in the age-old argument of the chicken and the egg, music would have to win. But it was my subsequent literary career, namely the book "Emissary of Light," that put me on the map. Till then I was a wandering troubadour playing my peace prayers for anyone who would listen. Sometimes that meant four or five people. Both seemed to be of equal importance for one would not exist without the other. Did it matter at all, or was the question itself an ego ploy to focus attention where it doesn't really belong.

To be honest, I often use both of these ventures, depending upon which one seems more important in a given moment, to advance the ultimate pursuit of the ego — specialness.

People have a tendency to measure their worth, as well as the worth of others, according to what they do rather than who they are. A lawyer deserves more respect than a dishwasher who works at the local diner, or so the world says. The ultimate excuse for such shortsighted vision is that a lawyer contributes more to society than a dishwasher. On the other hand, how many dishwasher jokes have you heard lately? The emphasis can obviously change in the blink of an eye, depending upon the desired goal.

I never know what to say when someone asks me what I do for a living. On a good day I'm tempted to look them straight in the eye and say, "What difference does it make," or "I work for the I.R.S., nice to meet you." Normally I opt for the obvious choice, but the question here is — what is the obvious choice? Once, when I was crossing the border into Canada, I realized that my profession definitely does make a difference. As I pulled up to the inspection booth and the guard asked me all of the standard questions, I felt we had a hint of rapport going. Then he asked me what I do for a living. "I'm a musician," I said. I was immediately ordered to pull my car over to the side for a thorough search. Who knows what sorts of illegal paraphernalia a musician might be trying to smuggle across the border. The next time I was in the same situation I smiled and said, "I'm an author." The response couldn't have been more different. The guard seemed impressed, smiled, and told me to have a nice day — all after I told him the title of one of my books so he could rush out and buy it.

If I had to choose one over the other I don't know what I would decide. I could never give up music, for that would be like cutting off an arm. But the process of writing a book stimulates me in a way that nothing else does. I've decided to consider myself blessed. There aren't many people in the world who are able to express themselves so freely and actually get paid for it.

So what was I doing in this mall, I wondered to myself. It was some deeper impulse that brought me here, some basic core issue that could not be answered so easily. Oh yes, music and books came easily to me, but settling down and getting married, that was a whole different story. The anticipation of this catastrophic shift had forced me inward, into myself and into the bowels of the mall where my retreat would serve to answer these questions. Or so I hoped. As I sat there on the bench I wondered if I was crazy. The first day of the retreat was drawing to a close and I was more confused than ever.

"Maybe I can sing my way out of this," one voice said.

"Better try writing your way free," the other voice echoed.

In the end, I decided it was best to head back to my guru — the shoe repair man.

"I see you have returned to hear more of my 'shoe philosophy'," the Shoe Man said. "Not many young people like you, I'm afraid, who can see the whole universe through the sole of a single person."

"Don't you mean 'soul'?" I asked.

"Please do not deprive me of my syntax. If we were speaking Chinese, I would amaze you with my language command. In English I need to settle for simple play on words. Please allow me this comfort."

"I will allow it."

"And why have you returned? Is it that you cannot wait for me to hire you and you want to learn my business now? You are either a saint or a thief. I have not decided which one."

"I'm really neither. I just wanted to talk some… to hear what you have to say… that is, if you're not too busy."

"As you can see, the shoe crowd has already left. What is it that you would have me remark."

"Well, you're here in the mall every day and you see so many different types of people. They're all unique and yet they're all the same. Do you know what I mean?"

"It is easy to see the differences in people, but it takes real vision to see the ways that we are all the same. I look at the world the same way I look at shoes. No pair is ever the same because they reflect the habits of the person who wears them. If you look at the bottom you can tell so much about a person… the way they walk, their posture… many things. But when you look inside it is always the same. The inside of the shoe is always soft, no matter who wore it. Even if the outside is cracked and dull, still the inside feels like wool."

"And you think people are the same way?"

"Inside, people are all the same because we all want the same things… peace, love, family. On the outside we are very different, the way we look and the way we talk. I am different than you because I come from China and you do not. But are we really so different. Maybe God doesn't think so either. Maybe God looks past the outer and sees only the inner."

"Like your shoes."

"Of course. Now, sometimes people don't realize what they want, and this causes confusion. They think they want pain or conflict, but that is only because they're used to these things. Ultimately we are all the same, with the same desires and hopes. Look past the confusion and you see the truth."

"You're like Confucius."

"No, I am just a shoe repair man. I only look around and see what is there."

"This sounds like a spiritual law to me — 'We are all the same regardless of the evidence.' Would you agree?"

"Regardless of the evidence… yes I like that. There is evidence for the mind and there is evidence for the heart. I'll choose the heart every time."

"So, how do we treat each other if we're all the same?"

"Think of it this way," he said. "We all want the same thing, though we don't always realize it. We all want love. Everything we ever do is either an act of love or a call for love. Right? If this is true, what should be our response to either situation?"

"Love."

"Yes, love. This is the key. Then we treat everyone the same, regardless of their actions. If someone brings their shoes to me with a smile, I smile back. If someone brings their shoes to me with a frown, I smile back. What they do does not matter at all. It is what I do that counts."

"Because you are the only one who will decide how you feel."

"Precisely," he said. "I like what you said before — 'Everyone is the same, regardless of the evidence.' That's all we need to be happy, isn't it?"

Lesson 3

Nothing Really Matters...
Anyone Can See

I was standing at the mall's main entrance when they unlocked the door at 9 a.m. the next morning. The insightful close to the previous day was enough to make me feel enthusiastic about the rest of my spiritual retreat. Each person I met that first day played an important role, just as one should expect. Bonds, which assist in one's experience, form on any retreat. There are the retreat guides, the fellow retreatants, as well as a few peripheral individuals that add color or intrigue to the mix. I had Peter the Jewelry Maker, the Coffee Man, the Shoe Man, the Hip Record Chick, and the Sour Book Lady, all in just one day. I couldn't wait to see what day two would bring.

I headed for Tim Horton's for a cup of coffee. As early as it was, I wasn't sure I wanted to start off the day with the Coffee Man. He was obviously intent on showing me the errors of my ways and would probably be weighted down with literature meant to save my wandering soul. Better to get some momentum behind me first, so just as I had the previous day, I decided to start off with Peter the jeweler.

"Good morning," he said as I walked through the door, coffee in hand. "I hope you're not here for the ring?"

"No. I'm just… well, shopping again. Thought I'd pop in and say hi."

"You sure do spend a lot of time in the mall. I hope you don't mind my saying this, but you don't seem like the mall type."

"What do you mean?" I asked.

"Well, there are three basic classes of people you'll find at any mall. I have to admit I've done some research on the subject. First of all, there are what we'll call the worker bees. These are people who are employed by one shop or another and who wander the halls whenever they're on break. You're not one of those. Second are what we'll call local color. This group can include mothers who need to get out of the house for a while, senior citizens who just want to be around other people, and other interesting specimens who simply don't fit into another category. Once again, you are clearly not of this group either. Finally, there are those who have a very particular mission to fulfill, the average person who knows what they want and are direct about finding it. I thought you were one of these, but the fact that you keep coming back excludes you from this class."

"What about people who are just plain shopping, not here every day, I mean, or even a couple times a week, but come in with the family for a few hours on Saturday?"

"We'll add them to the third group."

"There is one final group you should add to your list," I said.

"Yes?"

"It's a very small sample, one that would hardly register on your survey. And yet this small group could have a big impact, given the right circumstances, I mean."

"I'm listening."

"We'll call them researchers."

"Researchers?"

"Yes. As you said before, the mall offers a rich collection of social groups that would be an ideal laboratory for someone who wants to study, or learn. If someone were studying animals it makes sense for them to frequent the zoo, right?"

"I think you've gone too far."

"Why?"

"Well, as you said, this group would be so small it's hardly worth mentioning them. Unless, of course, this is your way of saying why you're here."

"Maybe."

"So what is it you're studying? The eating habits of the average Canadian mall shopper? Or is it the migratory patterns of post-pubescent teenagers who move from one side of the mall to the other, depending upon which side is darker."

"It's hard to say what I'm studying. Myself, I guess."

"Strange place to do it... in a mall."

"That's why I'm dong it here."

"You'll have to explain that one."

"I'll tell you what... I'll be hovering about for a few more days. Then I'll tell you what I discovered. If I were to say anything now it would contaminate my sample."

"Hey… I'm not going anywhere. In a few more days your ring will be done… wait a minute, I think I have a feeling what this is all about."

"Don't even go there."

"You know what I'm going to say?"

"Of course I do… I can see it in your eyes."

"Tell me I'm wrong then."

"Maybe the ring does have something to do with it, but only because it triggered something deeper."

"Engagement rings have a way of doing that, you know."

"I'm picking that up."

"Just remember that in the end, none of this will matter."

"None of what will matter?"

"Whatever it is you're going through. Everything passes, everything changes. What was tragic today is forgotten tomorrow. So study the mall, or yourself, all you want. In the end you will always return to where you started."

"And where is that?"

"Love. That's the business I'm in. These are symbols of love, these rings and necklaces. That's what we're all looking for, and it's where we all end up."

"That's very philosophical," I said. "Almost theological."

"I'm surrounded by gold and diamonds. What do you expect?"

I sat down at one of the benches in the food court to finish my coffee and decide if Peter was correct in his assessment of the mall population. I watched the people as they passed, big and small, young and old, and wondered if they really did fit into three neat categories. Are we so predictable that we can't even go to the mall without being pigeonholed? Are we so sad that this make-believe town is really a study in human relativism? I wanted to resist these notions as if they would destroy something essential about my own life. I may not fall into one of Peter's three main categories myself, but by defending these others I felt like I was defending something greater in us all, the chance to rise above stereotypes and the commonplace to the higher ground of individualism and democracy.

Or was I taking the whole thing too seriously? I was beginning to think that the introspection of this retreat was making me oversensitive. Why else would I be defending people whose lives were spent mall hopping, mall shopping, or mall flopping? I was there for one reason and one reason only — to go inside my soul and straighten out the clutter. Interactions along the way certainly played a part, but they were not the focus. Better to concentrate on the real goal and let the others fall into whatever categories they want.

The tables in the food court were arranged in tight rows, so tight that it was nearly impossible for one table to avoid contact with another. I had pried my way into the middle of one section as a sort of experiment. I wanted to be near these people, to breathe the same air they breathed. Maybe I would learn something about myself, some critical point where class separation loses its import. At first I thought my attitude was elitist, and I was willing to accept this sentence. In the end I decided that my willingness to ask such questions meant that I wasn't, in the same way that only a sane person can consider the possibility of insanity.

For the sake of full disclosure, I must admit at this point that I was eavesdropping. How else would I assess my own situation if not by the whims and prejudices of the people I had chosen as my retreat mates? They were the measuring sticks that would measure my own progress, my own spiritual advance. This was not a sin I was committing, but a necessary evil for one whose whole purpose was self-discovery.

Behind me sat a group of four old men. I had seen them the previous day, sitting in the very same place for a period of not less than four hours. I determined that this was "their mall," at least in their minds, the way anyone claims ownership of a thing because they use it the most. They were, at the very least, the "Grand Fathers" of Oakville Place, for their presence alone brought with it a certain stability that could not have been achieved otherwise. I tried not to be too obvious in my covert act. They actually made my job considerably easier than it needed to be, since I likely could have heard their voices three or four rows away.

"It is amazing how she treats me," the old Italian said, a man I later learned was named Renaldo. "You would think that after all these years she would trust my judgment. How many times have I been right about these things? Tell me, how many times?"

The man named Floyd hardly moved his face when he answered. "Many times." Through subsequent observation I learned he was from Poland, and his stone-like face reflected the stark realities of his previous life.

"Yes, many times," Renaldo continued, "So many times that I cannot count. You would think she would know this by now."

Renaldo was obviously the lord of this gathering of men. The others were welcome to add their own thoughts, opinions and paranoia, but Renaldo always set the agenda. His hands flew about so fast I was surprised that the Tim Horton's coffee remained on the table. There was an authority in his voice that the others never dared challenge. Even I was hypnotized by his certainty.

"Why do you put up with such behavior?" asked the man named Anthony. He was also Italian and served as Renaldo's guardian, watching his back, one could say, like an underling paying homage to the Mafioso boss. "You just say the word, Renaldo, and I'll have a talk with her."

"You just sit there and don't say a word," said Renaldo, challenged, not by Anthony's remark, but by the possible consequence of him speaking to his wife. "I don't need you making the situation worse. You speak to her, and next thing you know I pay the price. You just stay here and drink your coffee. That way you won't get me into trouble."

"Okay, Renaldo," Anthony said. "I'll do that."

Finally Marcus, the youngest of the group who I suspected was Greek, voiced his opinion. "You know what I think, Renaldo? Every day you come here and complain about your wife, then you go home and make nice with her. I don't think it matters what she does or what she says. The fact is, you wouldn't know what to do without her. The fact is she's the light of your life. Am I wrong? Nothing you say means anything because of that love."

This was a direct challenge to Renaldo's authority, but it was so calculated, so openhearted that there was nothing for him to do but agree. This, I was to learn, was Marcus' unique role. When all was said and done, after the men jabbed and sparred with any topic that came to mind, Marcus' reply was basically the same: None of that really matters, does it?"

"Yes, you are right," Renaldo said, dropping his guard for a period that did not exceed two seconds. "But my daughter... there is another story..."

And so the verbal barrage continued, shifting from one person to another. But no matter how intense the argument grew, how deliberate the attack, in the end they always ended at the same point.

"None of that really matters, does it, Renaldo? In the end only love matters."

The morning was shaping up nicely.

I decided to move toward the music store and see if my friend was working. After the men at the food court she would be a nice change. There was something about her open mood and honest composure that drew me in, not in a romantic sense but in a way that defied such license, an honest manner that didn't require reciprocity or exchange. She was able to relate to a whole area of my life in a way that no one else could in this mall. She spoke a language that transcends language, and that was a gift I was overjoyed to receive.

I walked in the door of the store and was happy to see her standing behind the counter.

"Mystery Man," she said as I stepped in front of her. "You're back. To what do I owe such a rare treat?"

"Well, you're the hippest chick in the mall... I think that's how you put it... and this is the hippest store. Seems like the perfect place for me."

"That must mean you're pretty hip as well," she said. "After all, hip attracts hip. It's the law of the universe, I think."

"I've never heard that one before, but it makes sense to me. How's business?"

"Considering it's 11 a.m. on Tuesday morning... not bad. I

think we've had five customers so far. I would include you but I don't consider you a customer.... Only a connoisseur."

"Much like yourself."

"You know it."

"I guess I'll have to buy something before I'm considered a customer."

"That's the way it normally works. I wouldn't be so fast though. It's rare when a person is both a customer and a connoisseur."

"Why is that?"

"Well, a connoisseur maintains a necessary distance, like a food critic or something. A food critic can never let on that they like a particular dish. It would be like showing your hand in a game of cards. They also never make friends with the restaurant owner."

"That means I shouldn't make friends with you."

"Yeah, but this is different."

"How's that?"

"Because I'm a connoisseur like you. Working here is only a front... Remember? I'm just saving up enough money to head toward Hollywood."

"Why Hollywood?"

"Well, actually Vancouver. But they're both on the west coast, so it's close enough."

"Okay, then why Vancouver?"

"Have you ever been there?"

"Yes. It's beautiful."

"That's why."

"Because it's beautiful. I guess that's good enough. Toronto's not bad either, but it's not beautiful like Vancouver."

"You know... Toronto's really not a bad city. If I lived in the city I would probably not be so quick to leave. It's just living out here in the burbs... enough to drive a hip chick like me nuts."

"I remember how that felt."

"How old are you anyway?" she asked.

"Thirty-eight going on thirty. Thirty-eight is obviously not that old, but it feels strange somehow. The years are just flying by, like my parents said they would. I didn't want to believe them."

"In the end, age is highly overrated."

"Why do you say that?"

"Think about it. You're thirty-eight and I'm twenty. You're almost twice my age. But does it really make much of a difference? You're hanging around this mall for God knows what reason, and yet you always seem to end up here talking to me. Why is that? Because we have something in common that transcends age, or years. Music is like that, perhaps more than anything else. Art maybe."

I listened to the music that was playing over the speakers — Queen's Bohemian Rhapsody. It caught my attention at the tail end, signaling one of the great lines in rock music.

"Nothing really matters, anyone can see. Nothing really matters... Nothing really matters to me."

"That sort of sums it up, don't you think?" I asked my friend.

"You mean Queen?"

"Yes. I heard a few old men say those same words a few minutes ago — 'Nothing really matters'. It's true when you think about it. Maybe that's one of the universal laws we're searching for. One of the old men said that, in the end, nothing really matters but love. Do you agree with that?"

"Hey, I'm a Beatles' fan. Of course I do. All you need is love, that's what I believe."

"So all the differences kind of fall away in the end, and what we're left with is something real, something revolutionary."

"You're starting to sound like Bob Dylan."

"That can't be bad."

"You ain't kidding."

"Nothing matters but love. That kind of puts it all in perspective."

"Speaking of perspective, I'd better get back to work. Got to head toward the back and unpack some boxes. But I have the feeling you'll be back."

"There's a solid chance of that."

"Good, you break the monotony of things around here."

"By the way," I said as she started to walk away, "what's your name?"

"You'll never guess."

"Okay."

"Penny… and my friends all call me Penny Lane. Cute, huh?"

I realized I was sitting outside the lingerie store staring at the scantily dressed mannequins, and jumped to attention. How did I get there, I wondered, without any conscious effort or foreshadowing? I had left the music store without any purposeful direction, wandered a bit in and out of various stores, then practically opened my eyes to find my full attention locked on a display of bras. How embarrassing. I looked around and tried to appear relaxed, hoping no one else noticed my long stay. As soon as I felt it was safe I resumed my curious inspection, hoping to discover the strange hypnotic pull it possessed.

Women entered, then left, and none of them registered an impression on my mind. There was something about the idea that transcended the reality... This is what attracted me, I'm sure. I didn't want to see a flesh and bone woman walk out of the store in a beautiful slip and bra, I wanted the freedom of creating the whole situation in my mind, the way I wanted it to be. That's the thing about obsession — it has very little to do with physical reality and a great deal to do with imagined reality. But imagination has its price. Before long I started to feel a wave of guilt rush through my veins. I hadn't done anything to be ashamed of, not in the physical sense, but what I did in my mind was just as blinding.

I stood up and walked away, suddenly disgusted with my behavior. After all, I was on a retreat, no matter how unconventional, and staring into a ladies underwear shop wasn't on the agenda. It was a lapse of judgment, and I whipped myself all the way down the hall.

But I remembered the lesson of the hour, the lesson I first heard from the old man in the food court, then again in the music store. "Nothing really matters... Anyone can see." How did that apply to my moral quandary? The same way it applies to everything else of course. I often say that only love is real. "Nothing really matters but love," as Marcus put it. If that's true, then there's nothing I can do to eclipse that perfect state. I can do anything I want and in the end it doesn't even matter.

Now, this is an issue we can debate forever. What about a murderer, or a rapist... their crime doesn't matter? In the end, no it doesn't, but that doesn't mean that we won't suffer from the results of our thoughts and our actions. All it means is that God's love for us is eternal, perfect. There's nothing we can do to screw it up. Love always prevails in the end.

What an optimistic viewpoint for someone who moments earlier used a crowbar to pry his attention away from the lingerie shop. If I can apply this rule to more serious indiscretions, then progress is certain. It seems such a simple lesson, but one that is regularly overlooked. Once it has been adopted, it must then overflow to others. That, I've learned, is the key to compassion. It's an inside out job, just like everything else of a spiritual nature.

As I walked toward the center of the mall, I saw the security guard from the day before standing beside a post scanning the crowd. At first I decided to stand apart and watch him for a moment, but not get too close lest he become suspicious. He was a serious man who took his job seriously. This had to be better than a guard who didn't take his job seriously, but perhaps not much better. I wondered if he was one of those overzealous types who took his enthusiasm a step or two past what was required. With his two fingers locked inside his belt, swaying from side to side, he reminded me of Barney Fife, though he was quite a bit bulkier. And though I figured it wasn't prudent, I knew I had to press the lesson I had just learned. Even if it meant risking my whole retreat, I had to talk to him again.

I approached him slowly so as not to disturb my prey. His attention was fixed on the 90 degrees or so in front of him, so I decided to approach from the left in his blind spot. If he spotted me too soon and remembered our previous encounter, it might startle him and he would spring into action. But if I could get close enough, perhaps to his side, before announcing myself, then there would be an opportunity for a breakthrough. I was halfway there and he still hadn't caught my scent. Thirty seconds later I was upon him, and I ventured forward to seal his fate.

"Hello officer," I said to him. "Hope you're having a good day."

He looked at me suspiciously, then his eyes widened when he remembered who I was.

"Yes, I am having a good day." Then he paused as if he wasn't sure what to make of the whole scene. I had confused him, this was obvious, for if I really was a troublemaker I wouldn't be so keen to establish contact. Or was there a deeper, more sinister motive in my mind — was I distracting him from something, some crime he was meant to miss? I could see all these things shoot through his mind as he looked at me, then looked around, then looked back at me again. "Is there something I can do for you, sir?"

"No, I just wanted to say hi. Our interaction yesterday was so fast I didn't get a chance to... Well, introduce myself properly. My name is Jimmy. And you're..."

"Sir, if it's all the same to you, I'd like to get back to my job. And please be careful... the security in this mall is very tight and we have an exemplary record in apprehending criminals."

I wasn't sure if he was trying to protect me, or warn me. Either way, I did have another motive in mind. I couldn't think of anyone I had met in the mall that I was more different from, and this seemed the perfect opportunity to practice what I had learned. No matter how different we were, we were essentially the same, at least in the areas that really matter.

"Thank you officer, I appreciate what you're doing here. Just so you know, I'm an author and I'm doing some research for a book. I didn't want you to get the wrong impression from yesterday."

His mood seemed to lighten and he became visibly more relaxed, like someone who suddenly realizes they're being filmed for Candid Camera. "Oh, I see... Yeah, you had me a little concerned yesterday, but I guess that's just part of your research, right? I wouldn't want to interfere with the creative process, you know. It just seemed kind of weird... Oh, never mind, no harm was done."

"I'm glad you understand. You like your job, don't you?"

"I love my job," he said. "I'm helping people, and that's all that's important. People need to know they're safe and can shop without fear. Some people think I take the whole thing kind of serious, but it's better than not taking it seriously at all."

"Yes, I know what you mean."

"I'm sure you take writing serious too, right?"

"Well, sometimes."

"You would have to. Are you a famous writer, like someone whose name I would recognize?"

"Probably not, sorry."

"Well maybe this will be the book that does it, the one you're researching now I mean."

"Yeah, I hope so. Well, I've taken up too much of your time already. I'd better let you get back to crime fighting."

"Okay then, it was nice talking to you."

I was humbled by the experience, but the lesson had been learned. We weren't that different after all.

Lesson 4

The Art of Divine Selfishness

It was nearly time for lunch and I wondered if the Coffee Man would be on break as he was the previous day. I stood near the entrance of the food court and scanned the crowd. The sea of humanity that was focused on satisfying that most basic hunger made me feel as if I was not alone in my sojourn. Whether they knew it or not, they were all on their own kind of retreat, for life itself is the real teacher, the real spiritual immersion. The mystic's path is simply realizing this fact: recognizing the immediacy of holiness and the urgency of awakening. Then the road opens and the signs all point toward the truth, regardless of one's definition. Truth, after all, cannot be limited to words, or concepts but is characterized by the experiences that lead one to joy. All these people were on the same path, though most were not conscious of this fact.

I finally found him sitting in the very same stool he had claimed the day before. For all I knew this was *his* stool, with his name engraved on a tiny metal slide. "Coffee Man", it reads, "Reserved." It didn't surprise me that he was a creature of habit. His job, after all, was to satisfy the public's craving for that bitter drink I love so, and which I know I must someday deny. I was struck, just as I was when I first saw him sitting there, at how alone he seemed. Even with all the people nudging their way into place, he was like an unaffected island, unaware of the storm that raged. I bought a sandwich and positioned myself in the booth across from him.

"Hello, Coffee Man," I said. "Good to see you again."

He seemed startled and looked up at me in a panic, as if he was afraid of what he would find. When he saw it was me he relaxed and sat back in his seat. "Oh, hello," he said. "You were here yesterday. Of course, you're the one I brought the literature for."

"Oh yes, the literature. I remember. You asked me if I was a Christian and didn't seem satisfied with my answer."

"It wasn't that I was unsatisfied," he said as he sat his sandwich on the paper bag, crushing it against the table. "I just wanted to give you a wider perspective… the fuller picture."

"Oh, I understand… that's why I'm here now."

"And that shows openness… the first step."

"Toward what?" I asked.

"What do you mean?"

"The first step toward what?"

"Well, toward the truth, of course. Isn't that what you're looking for?"

"Isn't that what we're all looking for?"

This question seemed to set him back for a moment, as if just for an instant he realized we were the same, regardless of our philosophical or religious differences. But then the well practiced lacquer returned and he continued his crusade.

"Of course we're all looking for truth. But how many of us find it... that's the real question. How many of us find the truth?"

"I guess we all do in the end," I said to him.

"What do you mean?"

"Well, I think that in the end the truth finds us... don't you think? We all may have different ways of getting there, some are fast and some are slow, but even a turtle arrives at the finish line in the end."

"A turtle?"

"Yeah, don't you remember..."

"Yes, of course, but it was a tortoise, not a turtle."

"Sorry."

"Anyway, it's not that simple. Some of us get lost along the way and never make it to the finish line. Just look at all these people... they're all preoccupied with survival and pleasure, they never consider the Lord."

"You mean Jesus?"

"Of course, Jesus. Jesus is the only way to truth. Without Him we're lost."

"I can agree with that to a certain point," I said.

"What do you mean?"

"Well, I love Jesus, just like I told you yesterday, and everything He taught. But was it His personality or his example we're meant to follow?"

"Both, of course."

"And for many that works fine, but there are others who make different choices or were raised differently. Now, when I was young I was taught that everyone has to accept Jesus or they're lost... going to hell. God might have mercy on a little African child that has never heard of Jesus but lives a good life, but if they're ever fortunate enough to hear His name and they don't follow, well, you know the end. Doesn't make much sense to me."

"Yes, but..."

I had the floor and I wasn't going to let it go quite yet. My passion was raised and I intended to make a clean run for the gate. "But that wouldn't be compassionate, and this, I believe, is one of the main attributes of God. How can God teach something He, or She, doesn't understand?"

"What are you saying?"

"That God is more than religion, and Jesus' message was more important than His personality. He gave us a blueprint, and if we want to be happy then we need to follow that blueprint. He taught us how to love one another, and how to be loved."

"And how would you describe that?"

"Give what you want."

"Give what you want?"

"Yes, this was His main message — giving and receiving are the same, so if you want something in your life, give that thing."

"But that's selfish."

"Why?"

"Because you're giving to get."

"In a way, yes, but what's wrong with that? Let's call it Divine Selfishness. It's really just about following universal laws, which are what Jesus taught. We all want love and peace in our lives, so what's wrong with giving it?"

"There isn't anything wrong with giving it."

"Then we agree?"

"No, not really, because we have left Jesus out."

"Why do you say that? How can you leave Jesus out when you dedicate your life to everything He taught? Didn't He say that you'll know a tree by the fruit that it bears?"

"Well… yes."

"So that's the answer… if you want love, give love. If you want peace, give peace. It's all so simple. Divine Selfishness. I think it's revolutionary."

There was a long pause as the Coffee Man looked into my eyes. I couldn't tell if he was with me or back at the beginning of the conversation. Then he began wrapping up the second half of his sandwich, brushed off his lap and stood to leave.

"And I thought I would preach to you," he said. "You've given me something to think about. Divine Selfishness. It's an interesting concept. Maybe there's something to it."

"Is that cappuccino you promised still available?" I asked as he walked away.

"Hey, if it's cappuccino I want, then it's cappuccino I give. Stop by anytime."

As I was walking away from the food court I saw my guru, the Shoe Man, walking toward his shop. I said hello and he grabbed me by the arm and led me in the direction he was walking.

"This is your lucky day," he said. "My assistant not coming in and I need your help. This will be the day you learn the fine art of shoe repair."

"But I'm…"

"No, you don't have to thank me. I know you've been here writing applications and making many interviews, but you don't need to continue now. I see the light in your eye, a necessary thing in my business because shoes are so important. You know what I mean, I'm sure. So today you begin."

I didn't know what to say, but I also didn't seem to have a choice. Before I knew what was happening I was in the shoe shop with an apron around my waist shining a pair of black dress shoes.

"I am so grateful for your help," the Shoe Man said. "With so many repairs I do not have time to shine."

"I'm glad I was walking by."

"This was no accident… do you realize that? Nothing happens by accident. You have need, and I have need. Now everyone is happy."

"I have need?"

"Of course. Why else would you fill out application?"

"Oh yes, of course," I said, but of course it went much deeper than he knew. He was right, not just about needing money. What I needed was help in moving from confusion into clarity. And that's what he needed, in a way. What a great opportunity to practice Divine Selfishness. I thought to myself, "Give what you need." I could feel my soul begin to shine along with the shoes.

"Yes… no accidents," the Shoe Man said again without looking up from his repair. "What you need, I give to you, and you give to me too. This is how the universe works, because it is by helping another that we ourselves are helped."

"It's funny, but I was just thinking that same thing," I said.

"It is a law, like the law of gravity. But this law does not pull us down, it pulls us up. When we forget our own needs and focus on helping others, then we find ourselves happy and we may even forget our lack because we are filled in a different way. Then the universe rushes in like water to fill all the gaps in our lives. When we focus on helping others, then we are helped in every way, often without asking or even knowing how the help came."

"You are very wise, Shoe Man."

"These things are so simple. It is a shame we forget how simple the truth is. My mother was very wise, a very respected woman in China when I was a boy. People came to her from all around our region and she would help them however she could. Sometimes she would give advice and other times she would give them some food. And always we had enough for ourselves, though we never had any money. I learned very much just by watching her live, and now I want to live in the same way."

"That's really why I'm here, to learn from you."

"And you come to learn more than shoe repair, don't you?" There was a glimmer in his eye as if he understood more than he let on. I wondered if I should tell him why I was really there. "Yes… you are here to learn about life, from an old Chinese shoe man. Well, everything you need to know is right in your hand."

"Tell me more."

He set down the shoe he was working on and walked over to where I stood. Then he rested his arm on the huge metal machine that does something, but I'm still not sure what, and took the shoe I was shining in both hands. "We are all like a pair of shoes walking through life. We start off shiny and new, then we're put on the ground and told to walk. We can't stay on the shelf all day, even though that's the only way we'll never get dust on our nice shiny finish, or get scuffed by the world. We have to experience things, and that means getting close to the earth, and the earth gets all over us. Before we know it, we're worn and scuffed and we may even have holes in our soles. But that's when the real challenge begins. We have to find ways to get off the ground and retreat for a bit. We take a rest and it's like being buffed with a nice soft cloth. Before you know it, the shine begins to come back and you can breathe again. Then we find someone we can trust who repairs the holes, giving us a new sole that can walk even further than before. Isn't that what life is like? We all need to slow down so we can keep our shine. Then we can help someone else."

"Because that's how we're helped... Give what you need."

"Yes, give what you need. That's very good. If we all gave what we need, then we would constantly be shining one another and fixing the holes in each other's soles. Then no one would ever lose their shine. It would reflect the sun so well that we would need to block our eyes."

"It's amazing what you can learn from a pair of shoes," I said to him.

"Life is my only teacher. It's all any of us need."

"Yes, this mall has been my teacher."

"Oh, a mall is a good place to learn about life. Everyone comes to the mall, though not always for the reason they think. People bring me their shoes but I try to give them more. Even a smile can change someone's life."

Lesson 5

The Practice of What is True

I arrived at the mall early the next morning filled with energy and enthusiasm. It was the third day of my five day retreat, which meant that by lunch time I would be half way home. As strange as it may have seemed on that first day when I called Karin to announce my unorthodox adventure, I was beginning to feel at home in the mall. Such a thought would have been distasteful at best, and I would have thought myself thin in the head. But how completely things had changed, all from a few conversations and insights. Maybe it was more than the mall but a statement about life itself. In the end we are not separated by miles, but by inches; not by insurmountable gaps but by a few simple thoughts. Change those thoughts and the whole universe collapses in around us.

In the event that the Shoe Man would rope me into service two days in a row, I decided to avoid him for awhile. His counsel was one of the highlights of my retreat, but there were so many others yet to explore. I would venture in his direction later in the day, after I had absorbed spiritual lessons on other fronts.

Instead I thought about the Book Lady I had toyed with on the first day, the woman who clung so tightly to her desk and seemed so afraid to venture out into the racks. Perhaps I had been too hard on her, I thought to myself. Instead of compassion, I had chosen to push her to the brink of disaster so that she ran back to familiar terrain. How cold and uncaring of me. I profess to be a spiritual teacher, someone who helps people face, then remove, the blocks of fear, but with her I had helped reinforce fear.

I sat down on a bench to consider my next move. Should I be direct and apologize for my actions? This seemed imprudent since she probably didn't realize my game. Better to turn the tide of my indiscretion and heal with gracious intent the wounds I had inflicted. I decided to do whatever I could, gently, to soothe rather than torment.

I could see her standing behind the counter as I stood outside the shop. It was as if she hadn't moved at all, but had her claws embedded so deep that it was impossible for her to leave. She scanned the store nervously and watched two or three customers browse the shelves. A young man walked up to her and seemed to ask for a particular title. She pointed in the direction of the rack and even motioned with a slight movement of her head, but never once moved from her post. I entered the store and acted as if I was looking at a book. Out of the corner of my eye I watched her, the bird perched upon a thin rod unable to fly, and I wondered what I would do.

Then I remembered one of my favorite lessons from the Shoe Man. He said that everything we ever do is an act of love or a call for love. Therefore, the only proper response in either situation is to give love. That's the answer. On our first meeting I offered her an attack, prying her away with force. I decided to change my approach and soothe her soul, coaxing her with a loving manner.

"Hi, I was hoping you could help me," I said to her.

There was a long pause while we looked at each other. I honestly didn't know what to say since I had approached the counter without any real plan. I figured it would all come to me in the moment, but at that moment nothing came at all.

"Yes?" she asked.

"Um, I was hoping you could order a book for me."

That was the first step, though I was flying without radar. Somehow I needed to create a bridge between normal bookstore talk and... whatever it was I set out to accomplish. But the goal was undefined and that made the action equally confused. Once again we stood there looking at each other.

"Are you sure we don't have the book you're looking for?" she asked in a gentle voice. "Here, let me check the stack. What book was it?"

"Uh, 'Portrait of the Master,' by James Twyman."

"Well, we have one book by that author, 'Emissary of Light,' but not the book you're looking for. Would you like me to order it for you now?"

I couldn't believe what was happening. This couldn't be the same person I had met two days earlier, the frightened woman who hardly said a word unless it was pulled out of her. I expected her to step out from behind the counter at any moment proving my previous experience was just a dream. She typed a few words on the computer and seconds later the deal was complete.

"There… it should be here in a week. Now what is your name so I can put it on reserve?"

She almost had me. I instinctively started to say my name, then realized the consequences if I did. Why would I be ordering my own book? This would surely bring us back to where we began, so I quickly made up an alias.

"Fred James," I said, combining my middle and given name.

"And a phone number."

"Well, I'm visiting town and don't remember my friend's number. Why don't I just stop by and pick it up in a week?"

"Fine. Here, let me check something." She stepped out from behind the counter and walked over to the shelf. Amazing. It was as natural as could be, none of the fear I had perceived before. I followed behind her just in case I learned something else.

"No… sorry… I thought I recognized the title. We just had a new stock come in and everything hasn't been entered yet."

"Oh, thanks for checking."

The Book Lady smiled and then walked back to the desk. I smiled back, then walked toward the door, looking for a place to consider what I had learned.

Here's the question I asked myself: Did the Book Lady change, or was it my perception of her? In two days her manner had completely shifted, and my judgments had to be tossed. The first day of my retreat I had established myself as her antagonist, and she responded perfectly. But then two days later I shifted to a different position, choosing to see her holiness instead. And as if by a miracle, her personality changed to accommodate my decision. It was as if she was a different person, or as if I was… I'm not sure which.

And if such a ploy can work with others, why can't we work such magic on ourselves? What would happen if we saw ourselves as the perfect beings we have always wanted to be? Would it be enough to shift the foundation of one's personality to reflect that perfection? Fake it till you make it... we've all heard that before. Maybe there's more wisdom in that than we thought. What if we're faking something that's already true? What a concept! And if it is already true, what does that mean? Perhaps it shows us that the former version, definition or concept we held of ourselves is the illusion, and the perfect version is the real truth. As I sat there on the bench looking at the woman standing at the counter, I could feel the tumblers falling into place. I decided to put my theory to the test.

I decided that I was enlightened. At first it felt good just to walk around the mall looking through the eyes of an enlightened being. I looked at everyone I passed and saw how beautiful they were, regardless of their appearance. There was no outward show or dramatic flair to what I did, just a feeling of peace that I tried to radiate, as if I wanted them to know how precious they were. After all, isn't that what an enlightened being does? I'm not talking about showboat enlightenment, the so-called master who makes sure the world knows they're enlightened. I've met people whom I was convinced had pierced the veil between this world and the next, who possessed a sense of inner certainty that could not be compromised by the outside world, but you would never have guessed them to be different. If anything, they were fully human in the truest sense of the word, holding clarity as if it were a diamond. That was the kind of enlightenment I wanted to practice, and even if I was faking it it made me feel great.

Or was it an act? The more I practiced this trick, the more I began to realize one of the most important spiritual lessons of all — We're already enlightened. The fact is that we've been faking *not being enlightened*, and we've gotten so good at it that we've forgotten the actual truth. We've been conditioned to think of ourselves as weak, vulnerable and alone, and it takes effort to break that spell and remember that such things are impossible. That's the first step to experiencing enlightenment, the realization that regardless of whether we're aware of it, it's still true. Then we begin the process of letting go of all the things that aren't true, and that may take some time. How many years have we been accumulating these untrue beliefs, all the dysfunctional attitudes that made the world what it is today? As I walked around the mall 'faking enlightenment', all these truths began to flood my mind as if they had been waiting to come out.

Several older women passed me and I gave them a wide smile. They seemed surprised at first, then turned around to look smiling back at me. This scene reoccurred over and over again as if the whole mall had been infected. And so it was. Just as I had discovered with the Book Lady, my attitude and thoughts were creating my reality. If I were to walk around the same mall at the same moment cursing the world and wearing a deep frown, no doubt I would see the same frowning world all around me. What an amazing discovery. We have heard this idea taught by many masters from around the world, but to actually experience it first hand is a completely different story.

It reminded me of the many times I had traveled to countries torn apart by war to perform the peace concert. I went to offer prayers in the places devastated by violence, often at the invitation of the government, and each time I found myself "looking for the war." Why? Because my intention was to demonstrate peace, to become peace, I seemed to attract peaceful situations wherever I went. When I was invited to Iraq by Saddam Hussein at the same time that US bombers were preparing a full scale assault, I thought I would be greeted with scorn. Instead, everyone I met was gracious, kind and happy to have me there. If I had gone there without such a strong intention, the situation might have been very different.

The enlightened me continued it's stroll of the mall. It made me wonder what would happen if we spent time everyday seeing with such vision. We normally see enlightenment in grandiose shades, as if it makes one special or better than others to see as God sees. But when we practice this ourselves it takes on a completely different tone. Enlightenment becomes ordinary — not in the ordinary sense of the word but in a way that makes the miraculous seem common. Miracles are natural when we adopt this mindset and are not seen as strange or uncommon. I discovered another wonderful byproduct of this practice — When you act as if you're enlightened, you begin to perceive others in the same manner. I call this "The Practice of What is True," and it became concrete for me that day. The fact is, we've been practicing what isn't true for a very long time. But when we change this trend and focus on seeing grace instead of sin, and peace instead of an attack, then the corresponding truth is drawn into our lives naturally, without effort. And what better place to practice this skill than in a busy mall?

I decided to let the third day of my retreat be a "Day for Enlightenment." I spent hours watching people, and watching myself. All in all, it was one of the most productive times I can remember. After all, practicing what isn't true takes a great deal of effort. Turn the tables on yourself and you may be surprised at how simple enlightenment really is.

Lesson 6

God Doesn't Care
What You Do...
(but rather, who you are)

It was time to take the Coffee Man up on his offer of a free latte. The day was passing quickly and the adrenaline lift of a strong cup of coffee was just what I needed. The practice of being enlightened had sent me flying through the mall, and though it was an invigorating experience I started to crave the feel of solid earth again. And besides, I was sure the Coffee Man wasn't finished with me yet, nor me with him.

"Hello there," he said as I entered the shop. His mood seemed so much higher than the two previous days. Was it him, or was it another miracle caused by my newly discovered enlightenment?

"Hello, Coffee Man," I said. "You know, you never actually gave me the literature you promised before. I was hoping I hadn't scared you off."

"Far from it. Our conversation really got me thinking, especially about compassion. I hate to admit it, but it's making me re-think a lot of things."

"Why do you hate to admit that?"

"Well, a person likes to think he understands a few things, that there are a few constancies in their life. But sometimes we get locked into certain ideas about the truth, and then we lose track of the truth itself. Ideas aren't the goal after all, are they? It's truth itself we're after, and that takes an open mind."

"You're turning into a philosopher."

"Maybe I am," he continued. "I've never been one for philosophy. I've always done what I was told and believed what was put in front of me. Don't get me wrong, though. I'm not backing away from anything, just looking at it with an open mind."

"There's nothing wrong with that."

"How could there be. It's like you said yesterday — God loves us and that can't change. That's what compassion is, after all.

"I said that?"

"Or something like that. It makes sense when you think about it."

"So, are you saying that God doesn't care what we do?"

Coffee Man had to think about this one for a moment. He was talking so fast he didn't want to get ahead of himself, as if he didn't want to say something he couldn't take back later.

This was a big jump for him. He had come a long way in discovering how vast God's love and compassion are, but the new idea I proposed was definitely a step out on a limb.

"Well, I'm not sure about that one," he finally said. "Of course God cares what we do. Why wouldn't He?"

"Or She."

"Whatever, just answer the question."

"Well, what if there's something that's more important? We've gotten to the place where we can admit that God's compassion is eternal… it seems to me that this is the natural next step."

"But that would mean we can do anything we want and it wouldn't matter. We can kill and rape and God looks the other way?

"I'm not saying that."

"Then what are you saying?"

"Only that there's something that's more important… like who we are… the truth in us."

He set my latte on the counter and was able to really digest what I was saying. Luckily the mall was nearly deserted and no one entered the café while I was there, almost as if the angels were helping keep the coast clear.

"And what does that mean?" he asked with an intense stare.

"Well, God made and loves us, right? We are made from the same Divine substance as God, since nothing can be truly separate from what is all pervading. That would mean that God's attention is always focused on the truth in us, not the illusion. We, on the other hand, tend to focus on what isn't real, like separation and death, and from that comes all sorts of distortion. But if God's vision is unwavering, then none of that really matters. All that really matters is the truth."

I could see the Coffee Man trying to grasp what I was saying, but his rational mind rebelled. "But it still doesn't make sense," he said. "That would make sin okay, as if we don't need to be forgiven."

"But I'm not saying that."

"It sure sounds like you are."

"We can't avoid the laws of this world as long as we are in this world," I said, "and one of those laws is that for every action there is an equal and opposite reaction. This applies to the spiritual universe as well as the physical universe. If we do good in the world then we tend to draw goodness into our lives. But when we do evil the same eventually comes back to us. But does that mean that we're being punished by God, or that we're just suffering from the effects of our own actions? If the first were true then that means God loves Mother Teresa but hates Hitler. Once again, this would mean that God is without compassion. What if God loves Hitler as much as Mother Teresa, but has given each the free will to create their life experience? Hitler loved darkness and so attracted more darkness into his life. In the end it overwhelmed and killed him. Mother Teresa, on the other hand, dedicated her life to service and love, and in doing so she attracted the admiration of the whole world. Is it possible that God never paid attention to anything but the truth in them both?"

"But that would be... would be...?"

"Revolutionary," I said, completing his sentence. "It would mean that God doesn't care what we do — but who we are. It would mean that God is the essence of compassion because nothing interrupts His, or Her, vision of the truth."

"But everyone does sin," he said, grasping for spiritual straws.

"Of course we do," I said, finally taking a sip of the latte. "So what... We all make mistakes. I believe that we're all being called to See as God Sees and focus on the truth rather than sin. We're here to learn the same compassion that God practices all the time."

"Why is it that every time I see you and I'm thinking I'm going to teach you something, you always turn the tables and it's me who gets preached to?"

"I'm not sure," I said. "Does it really matter?"

"I guess it doesn't since we're both pointed in the same direction."

"That's right. We're both pointed in the same direction. I like that."

I took my latte and returned to the food court to consider everything I just said. I have realized in the past how important it is for me to listen to the words that come out of my own mouth. This is a good lesson for everyone, I've decided. We often say things to others that we ourselves would do well to heed. I often say that we teach what we most need to learn. This is the single reason I spend so much time talking about peace — because peace is ultimately all I want in my life. "For it is in giving that we receive," the Prayer of St. Francis says. I wasn't there to teach Coffee Man anything at all, but myself.

As I stood looking for a seat I spotted my friends, the four old men I had never actually met but on whom I had eavesdropped two days earlier. They were sitting in the exact same place, in the exact same order, as they had before. And on their faces I sensed the same certitude, the possessive attitudes that made one feel they were intruding in someone else's home. Lucky for me that the seat I had previously occupied was free as well. I sat down to listen.

"It's hard to believe he can get away with such a crime," Renaldo said to the others. "What the hell was he thinking, anyway? What could have possessed him?"

"It's a good question, Renaldo," Anthony said. "A good question."

"Of course it's a good question," Renaldo continued. "What do you think I've been saying all this time? That guy is trouble... I said it before and I'll say it again."

"So what are we going to do?" Floyd asked without moving his mouth at all.

"We're not going to do anything," put in Marcus. "What do you think, that we're going to interfere? Not a chance."

"What do you mean, we're not going to do anything?" Renaldo asked, reestablishing control. "Since when do you make decisions, Marcus? We're most definitely going to do something."

"And what is it we're going to do?" Marcus countered. "All we ever do is sit here and talk about all this big stuff, but all we do is sit here and talk. Maybe if we got off our butts, but not till then."

I realized that I had absolutely no idea what they were talking about. All I could gather is that someone they all knew had done something that did not meet with their approval, but they were at odds as to their potential action. I wanted to say something to them, to lean over and tell them about my discussion with Coffee Man. Instead, I decided to listen further and see what new wisdom I could glean.

"You have no right to talk to us that way," Anthony said to Marcus. "Something's got to be done by someone... why not us?"

"Why not let the guy live his life the way he wants to?" Marcus said. "Haven't we all made mistakes? How would you like a bunch of old farts like us breathing down your neck every time you make a wrong turn?"

"You don't understand," Renaldo said as he leaned into the table. "This isn't the first time. He needs to be taught a lesson."

"We're the ones who need to be taught a lesson. The guy made a few mistakes. Who do you think you are, Renaldo — God?"

At that point I knew we were going somewhere.

"Well, if I was God I wouldn't sit around and wait for him..."

"If you were God, you would reach down from Heaven and touch him on the head real nice and then you would turn around and smack the four of us on the ass. Yeah, I'm pretty sure that's what you would do."

The conversation continued moving in this general direction till the men got tired and moved on to another subject. But the lesson had been learned. Sometimes we all need a little smack on the butt, and a whole lot of compassion. But most of all we need to look a little deeper than we're prone to looking. Who knows what we'll all see? Maybe that we're not so different from one another after all. Then, just maybe, that realization will lead to something deeper - that it doesn't really matter what we do. What matters is that we do not forget who we are.

It was time to return to the Shoe Man. It had been an amazing, insightful day and I knew that there was only one way to tie it all together in a neat little bow. The day had been spent practicing what is true, and realizing that God cares a whole lot more about who we are than what we do. The Shoe Man was sure to have something to say about these subjects. He saw me walking toward his shop and an enormous smile illumined his face.

"It is my good friend coming to help... oh, but not today. It has been so slow and I have already finished everything."

"That's okay, Shoe Man. I was just getting ready to leave but I wanted to stop by and say hello."

"I have been meaning to ask you something," Shoe Man said to me. "What are you really doing in this mall? You have not come looking for a job, or else you would have found one by now. I sense there is some deeper motive, as if you are here to learn about who you are, not what you do."

"That's an amazing observation," I said to him. "It's exactly what I've been thinking about today. To answer your question, I'm here just watching — myself and others, learning whatever the mall has to teach me. It's kind of a retreat."

"A retreat - in the mall?"

"Yes, in a way it is... in fact I think it's the perfect place for a retreat, and I'm sure you understand that better than anyone. Where else can we watch and observe, discovering what we cling to and what we love? This is where average people come to be who they are, in a place where you can blend into the crowd and find whatever you want. I've gone on retreats in many places — in monasteries, spiritual centers... but after three days I've learned more here than in all of them combined."

"Tell me what you have learned today."

"I've learned that God doesn't care what we do, but focuses on who we are. We are all holy and blessed regardless of what we do or how we behave. Our actions may certainly slow down our spiritual evolution, but that doesn't reflect how much God loves us. And it is up to us to initiate that same attitude. I think that this is the key to forgiveness and compassion."

"You know, I was raised Buddhist," Shoe Man said, "and that does not acknowledge a personal God like many other religions. But we believe that all life is filled and refilled by the sacred waters that ultimately wash us into the Ocean of Divinity. All life is sacred, which is what you are now describing. If we focus on this every moment of every day, no matter where we are or what we are doing, then life begins to make sense.

"I stand here all day long shining other peoples' shoes," Shoe Man continued. "But that is only what it looks like I am doing. In reality I am shining my own soul. I look out at the people who pass or the customers who come into my shop, and I try to remember how holy they are. And that reminds me how holy I am, for we are one, regardless of what we do. You are right… this is the perfect place for a retreat, not removed from the world. I say, dive right into the river and let the current take you where it will. This is the best way to live because the river has it's own lessons to teach us, and we learn them by being willing to swim."

"So I guess I've dived into the mall, and it's leading to places I didn't expect."

"That is the beauty of life," he said. "We can never really expect anything, but we can move with what is right in front of us. I'm sure your retreat has many more lessons to teach you,"

"I'm sure you're right, Shoe Man. I'm sure you're right."

Lesson 7

The Declaration of Dependence

I returned the next morning to begin my fourth day. Arriving early, before most people, was in itself an opportunity. Many of the shops were just beginning to open their doors and in the food court preparations were being made for the busy day. A few customers rummaged about looking in windows or pushing children in strollers, and the four old men arrived on schedule to stake their claim to their favorite table. I was beginning to feel like I belonged there, as if I was getting used to the rhythm. I could almost predict what would happen next or which employees would be in which stores. Before long I was standing in front of Raffe Jewelers and saw Peter unlocking the door.

"Well hello," he said to me. "It must be two days since you were here last. I was beginning to wonder what had happened. Just so you know, your ring should be ready tomorrow, and it's going to look beautiful."

"Oh, that's fantastic," I answered. "That means my retreat will finally be over... or, I can finally give it to Siri Rishi."

"Your retreat... what do you mean?"

"Well, if you must know, ever since I came here a week ago I've been sort of studying myself — like a retreat. I used to despise malls and avoid them at all cost. Then I came here to buy the ring and something happened to me. It really threw me for a loop and I realized I had two choices. I could run from the fear and deny it, or I could dive right into it and see where it would lead. I've been coming here everyday since then, and I've been learning some amazing lessons, all because I bought a ring from you."

"So, you think it was because of a ring?" Peter asked.

"Well, indirectly of course. The ring was like a trigger that taught me a few things about myself. I didn't realize how afraid I was to really commit to a relationship till I came here. The fact is, I feel much better now, and as soon as I get the ring the retreat will be over."

"Why don't you come inside for a moment," Peter said. "I want to show you something."

He led me behind the counter into a small room in the back. In the corner there was a large table with lights and tools, and dozens of small containers filled with diamonds and jewels.

"This is where my brother spends most of his time," he said. "Making all the jewelry you see out there in the cases. I'm the front man selling what he makes. It works out good that way. But it's here in the back room that the real magic happens. This is where the dreams come together. People come into the store with an idea, something they have in their mind, barely more than a thought, and then my brother has to turn that thought into a ring, or a necklace, or whatever.

"When you and your fiancée came here, you knew you wanted a ring to symbolize your commitment and love. Then it came here, to the back room, where the diamonds are placed in a certain order and set in gold, then ultimately, tomorrow, it comes back to the front where you get to finally see how it looks."

"Is this like the conscious and the unconscious mind?" I asked him.

"Sure, in a way. You had all this fear inside you, but it wasn't conscious till the order for the ring went to the back room. While my brother's been making your ring, you've been walking around the mall sorting through all the fears and worries. But the ring is nearly done, and so are your lessons. They've been brewing in your unconscious till you were ready. One more day to go and it's through."

"You mean, I'm through."

"No, you're not through. We're never through... We just move on to higher lessons, brighter diamonds."

"You know, the thing I love the most about this mall is that every store has its own lessons to teach. Where did you get so wise, anyway?"

"In California."

"California?"

"Yeah, I used to live in Berkley when I was a kid, then the family moved up to Canada. I used to take classes there, philosophy mainly and, you know, life teaches you certain lessons. California is great for that."

"I know... I live there now."

"Then you know. Here's something for you to think about — What you're really afraid of, in my opinion, is giving up your independence. That's what the ring symbolizes. But when you think about it, it's not independence that gives us freedom, but dependence."

"What do you mean?"

"When I lived in the States I learned about the Declaration of Independence, the document that cut your country's ties with England. That may be fine for a country, but people aren't meant to be alone, or independent. Growth occurs when we learn to depend on one another, and when they depend on us. We have to support one another, and that's how we end up being supported as well. It works both ways, you know."

"So, we need to make a Declaration of Dependence," I said.

"That's what you're doing by buying this ring. And all the lessons you're learning are like placing the diamonds in a neat row. In the end you'll have a beautiful piece of jewelry."

"That's quite a metaphor."

"It's really more than a metaphor," he continued. "It's what life is all about."

"One step further," I added. "When we learn to depend on one another it's one step closer to depending on God."

"That makes sense."

"You could say that we declared our independence from God, but now we're learning to turn around and reestablish contact. When we depend upon God for everything, then everything is ours."

"Sort of like the center diamond," Peter said.

"It all comes back to diamonds with you, doesn't it?" I asked.

"That's what I know, but it all applies to the real world."

"I guess that's the key, that we use it all to learn about ourselves."

In the center of the mall the finishing touches were being put on Santa Claus' temporary residence, the tiny village where holiday cheer is resurrected each year around Thanksgiving. I watched the children's faces as they passed, looks of anticipation and awe. In a few more days he would be there, the mother's were saying... then you can tell Santa everything you want. If only life could have stayed that simple, that fantastic. Sometimes I wish I had never stopped believing in Santa.

I remembered when my own daughter Angela was about three years old and I was asked to dress up as Santa Claus one Saturday afternoon. The man that had been hired for the job was sick and my friend who managed the mall thought it would be a fun experience for me. I have to admit that the prospect stirred my interest, and before I knew it I was dressed and ready to go, equipped with a bag full of candy canes and a healthy "Ho, Ho, Ho."

I called Linda, my former wife, and asked her to bring Angela to the store. Visiting Santa was all she had been able to think about for weeks, and her list had already grown considerably. Wouldn't it be great to have Angela's picture taken with "Daddy Santa," I said to Linda, then look back years later when she's old enough to understand? It seemed like a great plan, but it ended up teaching me a very valuable lesson that extended past the white beard and red suit I was wearing.

I was sitting in the chair surrounded by children when I saw Angela and Linda enter the store. Angela looked like a scared little rabbit as she held onto her mother's hand, as if letting go would expose her to some tragic and unforeseen fate. But "Daddy Santa" knew exactly what she needed. As soon as she saw me standing there, disguised as the great Christmas gift giver, she was sure to come alive and rush toward me with her arms open wide.

I stood up from my oversized chair, looked toward my daughter and said in a booming voice, "Ho, Ho, Ho, hello Angela."

I couldn't have been more surprised by her reaction. She let out a scream that could be heard from one side of the huge store to the other. Linda didn't know what to do and was as surprised as I was. Angela buried her head in her mother's stomach and seemed absolutely terrorized. No matter what happened next, she wasn't about to take another step toward that frightening man with the white beard, even if she had come there to see him.

After about a minute of this, which had of course attracted the attention of nearly everyone in the store, I decided to make my move. In retrospect, I'm not sure if this was the most skillful move on my part, but something had to be done. Angela's head was still buried in Linda's stomach and she couldn't see me as I left my assigned position and came over to her. When she finally turned and saw me standing there she nearly fainted. Her mouth opened wide and her scream was so intense that no sound came out at all. This would be the moment of truth, I realized. Either we deal with this situation or she would be forever scarred.

I fell to my knees in front of her. Then I did whatever I had to do to get her to look at me, if only for a few seconds. It was all I needed, for I knew what my next move would be. She finally opened her eyes and braved a quick glance in my direction. Our eyes locked, and when they did I launched into action. I pulled the beard down, looked at her sympathetically and said, "Angela, it's just Daddy."

I could see the little wheels turning in her brain. This information did not compute and there was no way to wrap her mind around what she had just heard, "Daddy is Santa? Santa is Daddy?" But then her eyes brightened and I could see she understood. "It's just Daddy. I don't need to be afraid of Daddy. Daddy loves me." The fear was gone and everything was okay.

Sitting there in the mall watching Santa's Village being constructed, I could see the parallel between this story and my discussion with Peter. No matter what we say or how long our list may become, we have become afraid of God. Most of us were raised with images of the "Great Father in the Sky" that resembled Santa Claus more than the Supreme Being. We talk about God and we go to church and pray, but it really isn't until we release our declaration of independence that we face the fear. We're afraid we did something wrong by turning away, and we believe we're going to be punished for that offense. It's not until the beard comes down and we realize that it's just Daddy that the anxiety dissipates and we realize that there's nothing to fear after all. Then we can relax and be dependent again, just like a little child. And that's when life really begins.

Peter was right again.

Lesson 8

Change is Not Necessary

I had been on my mall retreat for nearly four days and it felt like a good time to reflect on the many lessons I had learned. I entered those sacred passages like a novice and would leave a great deal more experienced, if not even wiser. Who would have thought that I could find enlightenment in such commercial upheaval? More than anything I had learned that it's the situations and places we most resist that often offer the greatest gift. To hold a spiritual experience in the tight constraints of a traditional retreat would serve, but it felt as if I had stumbled upon something grander, more real than I could have imagined. Each lesson was etched on the faces of the ordinary people I met. I would have once separated myself from these others, as if they existed in a whole different world. Now I realized that we are the same in those essential elements that

God perceives. I realized that all my mistakes combined were not nearly as potent as God's love for me. I had even learned the benefits of spiritual selfishness, and the declaration of dependence. So many lessons in such a short period of time, and in such a strange place. I can absorb them because of the decision I made to see myself as a perfect being. Every person I meet is affected and I carry them with me.

I decided I would use the opportunity to catch up on my Christmas shopping. This, of course, is the equivalent of the World Series at any mall. The stores prepare and decorate, all to cash in on the general public's Yuletide cheer. Come January the traffic will fade and the well-intentioned enthusiasm will have passed, so they might as well take advantage of it while they can. The atmosphere was relaxed and calm, but there was an electricity in the air that I could taste, as if there were wires plugged into the backs of everyone present, filling them with an unseen energy. People buzzed from one store to another like windup toys and yet the smell of Christmas wafted through the air like fine incense.

I had already spent the Canadian cash I carried and decided to visit the bank outlet near the entrance to change more U.S. dollars. I stood in line and could feel something moving inside me, as if another insight was about to fall into my lap, another wonderful lesson to put into the stocking hanging over my chimney. I looked around trying to anticipate its approach, but the solemn group around me offered little inspiration. Within minutes the line moved forward and it was my turn to be served.

"I'd like to change $100 U.S. to Canadian dollars," I said to the young man behind the counter.

"No problem," he said as he took the bills from my hand and began typing on his computer keypad. I waited patiently till he was finished and the printer provided the forms to sign. "Can you sign here?" he said, pointing to the line.

"Of course," I answered, and then signed. Then he looked up at the screen as if he was confused, as if he was unsure how he should proceed. I had seen this before. Sometimes the exchange is not exact and the cashier asks if you have any change to round things off. I didn't even wait for the question but offered — "Do you need more change?"

"Oh no!" he said. "*Change is not required.*"

It was as if the room went blank and I was shot into a dream. Those words, that offhand remark, hit me right between the eyes and sent me flying. I obviously knew what he meant, but there was deeper meaning as well, and it was this that drew my attention.

"What did you say?" I asked him.

"I said that no change is required. I was just looking for something on the screen, but I've found it now."

"Are you sure?" I asked. "No change is required... could that be true?"

He looked at me puzzled and wondered what I was talking about. "I'm not sure what it is you're asking, sir."

"About change... you said that no change is required. Don't you think that's amazing?"

"Why would I?"

"Because we're perfect just the way we are, right? We don't need to change... we just need to accept who we really are. We always think we need to change... but we don't. That's what you were saying... I'm sure of it."

"Sir, there are people waiting in line. Is there anything else I can do for you?"

"Of course not, you've already done more than you can

imagine. You're like this amazing cosmic Santa Claus who gave me exactly what I needed."

"That's great, sir, but…"

"Oh, don't worry, I'm leaving. I just wanted you to know… Oh, never mind."

I danced out of the bank and into the mall. The eighth lesson had suddenly arrived.

I returned to the food court and stood near the escalator where I could see the sign, "Change is available at the Concierge Desk." I remembered the scene I had made on the first day of my retreat when I pushed the validity of this sign. It was nearly the cause of my expulsion, but everything was different now. I was approaching the end of day four, and my epiphany in the bank urged me to keep moving forward.

But I certainly wasn't going to make the same mistake and rush forward before I had a plan. I stood back from the desk, sheltered by several artificial trees that made me feel like a confused squirrel or raccoon, and waited for the right moment. My friend the security guard stood near the desk just as he had on Monday, and I could feel my breath growing quick and heavy. Would this be the final insight I would learn before being finally and permanently removed from my retreat? Or was there a deeper force at work, one that would protect me from my own overextended fervor? There was still time to push back and seek another lesson in another area of the mall, but I knew I wouldn't. It was time to risk it all, to walk out on the limb further than I perhaps should. How else would I learn my lesson if not through danger and risk?

That was when my big break came. The guard nodded his

head at the woman behind the counter, wrapped his fingers around his billie club, then walked away. He was off to another side of the mall to make his presence known. I took this as my sign to move into action. Alone, the woman did not present such a problem, even if I did decide to push my point again. One way or another, I was going to learn everything I could about change, and the fact that none is required.

It was a different woman than the one I had encountered days earlier. Her eyes scanned the crowd, hoping to connect with someone who could use her help. When I was still a few steps away from her desk, our eyes met and her smile widened.

"Hello, and Happy Holidays," she beamed. "How can I help you today?"

Her effervescence took me by surprise and all my fear vanished. I could sense that she was very much like me, using this human playground to express something deeper than normal, or to learn something deeper about herself. I smiled back and stepped up to the desk.

"Yes," I said to her, "I would like your opinion on something. You sit here all day long watching and helping people. Do you believe that there is something in them all that is the same, or that transcends their differences? I know it's a strange question, but I was…"

"No, it's not strange at all," she said. "Well, maybe a little, but I don't mind. I love my job because I get to meet so many nice people, even when they're not. I talk to people all the time who are so interesting, even when they're not interesting at all."

"What do you mean?"

"Well, of course people come here when they're upset or lost, but I try to look past all that to that very quiet place inside them… Oh, I need to listen to myself before I say things. Why, you must think I'm crazy."

No, you're not crazy, I thought. "Actually you're saying exactly what I came to hear," I said. "So you think that there is something inside of us that can't change, that doesn't need to change, and that's the thing that unites us, even when we don't realize it?"

"That's a very good way of saying it. Call me old-fashioned, but I think that people are essentially good inside, even when they don't act like it. Of course we all do things we're not proud of, and we all have regrets, but in spite of it all we don't need to change a thing because God loves us no matter what."

"You really believe that?" I asked.

"Yes, I do. You know, I don't even need this job. I took it because it gives me the chance to smile at people and tell them how wonderful they are. I retired from teaching about five years ago, so this is what I do with my retirement."

"What grade did you teach?"

"I taught seventh grade, so I know a thing or two about seeing past the nonsense. Do you remember when you were in seventh grade?"

"How could I forget? It was like being in hell."

"But now look at you," she continued. "You're all grown up and writing books."

"How did you know I'm a writer?"

"The security guard told me there was a writer doing research in the mall, and when you started asking unusual questions, well, I put two and two together."

"I wish I had met you a few days ago," I said.

"Why?"

"Because I could have used your insight on my first couple of days."

"We met exactly when we were meant to meet. I wouldn't change a thing."

"Are you sure about that?" I asked.

"Positive."

I walked again through the food court and past the Shoe Man's shop. He was busy polishing a pair of black shoes when he looked up at me and smiled. I smiled back and raised my hand. Then he went back to his work and continued polishing the shoes till he could see his own face reflecting back at him.

I set off to do the same thing to my soul.

Lesson 9

God is Rather Ordinary

THE FINAL DAY

I sat on my normal bench in the food court, sipping a cup of coffee and watching the two men like a detective. No one would have ever known I was there or that I was studying them so intently. If it was not so strange, so surreal, I would have certainly looked away, but the scene was so captivating that there was nothing I could do but watch.

Sitting on a bench to my side was an old man with white hair and a bushy white beard. Even if he didn't have a nine-inch statue of Santa Claus sitting in front of him on the table he would have still certainly passed as the merry gift giver. Across from me in the open area in the center of the mall, the "other"

Santa Claus sat in his huge red chair greeting children and handing out candy canes. The exit from "Santa's Village" led straight into the food court where, of course, the man at my side was sitting with his statuette. I could see the confusion in the eyes of the children when they walked away from the traditional Santa right into "Plain Clothes" Santa. And then he would laugh, a low Santa Claus sort of laugh, and suddenly the statue came to life. Everyone stood in amazement as it did a little jig, its bottom end wiggling back and forth and its belly wiggling up and down as if it were, well... filled with jelly.

If I were still a child such an encounter would have confused me beyond words. One enters a kingdom with cotton instead of snow, and plastic hanging lights instead of icicles, and are told to sit on Santa's lap. No wonder my own daughter had been so traumatized. Then imagine leaving that village and walking right into another version of the same reality, different, perhaps even warped, but more real than the other. Take away the butt-jiggling statuette and what you're left with is a down-to-earth Kris Kringle that is little more than ordinary.

What lesson can I learn from this, I wondered? If my retreat taught me anything it was to find the Divine through the ordinary, not the extraordinary. We spend so much of our time waiting for lightning bolts that we often miss God when he, or she, is right in front of us. The glitz and glamour actually blinds us to what is more essential. And we tend to prefer the imagined to the real. The kids are lined up in front of Santa's Village and sit proudly on Santa's lap as they recite lists of "I want this," or "I want that." But all the while the real Santa sits a few feet away smiling and dancing and confusing older children like me.

I wanted to say something to the real Santa Claus, but I decided not to. He was having fun raising eyebrows with his loud laugh and dancing miniature self. Let him have his fun, I said to myself. Santa deserves a laugh now and then.

"What's up, Author Man?"

I turned and saw the Hip Chick from the record store walking toward me, and before I knew it she was sitting on the other side of the bench staring into my eyes.

"How did you know I was an author?" I asked her. "Don't tell me, it was the security guard wasn't it?"

"You bet. He's telling everyone that there's a famous author hanging around writing a book, asking all sorts of crazy questions. I knew right away it must be you. So tell me, am I in your book? Is there room for a gorgeous, insightful sales lady with great taste in music?"

"There might be," I said. "You've actually helped me with your insights without you even knowing it."

"Oh, I knew it."

"How?"

"I may be young, but that doesn't make me stupid."

"That's obvious."

"My friends always come to me with their problems, and I always have something to say."

"Does it help?"

"Of course it helps, especially when their problems are about music… which doesn't happen very often."

"I suppose it wouldn't."

"So tell me, who else is in your book? Are you, like, going around the mall writing about the people you meet and the gossip you hear?"

"Kind of, yes, but there isn't much gossip."

"Then you're not listening. There's a lot of gossip in this mall."

"Mainly I'm listening to people, ordinary people, and learning extraordinary lessons about them."

"That sounds kind of boring," she said.

"It's not, in fact I'm discovering a whole ocean of opportunity in the ordinary. Take you, for example..."

"Before you go any further, I'm anything but ordinary."

"In some ways yes, but take away the charming little differences and we're all the same. I'm learning to focus on that sameness and to make it more important than the differences. This mall is the perfect place to do that. There are so many different sorts of people here, and it's tempting to think we're all very unique. But in the end we all want the same things in our lives. We all want to love and be loved, to discover what lies beneath all these layers of superficial differences."

"So, it's a book about philosophy. Sounds exciting."

"No, not philosophy... way deeper than that. It's about ordinary life, and finding the sacred in it."

"So it's a book about God?"

"Sort of... about finding God everywhere."

"Even in a mall?"

"Especially in a mall. That's where I met you, and so many others. The more I talk to them, the more I learn about myself. I guess that's the real reason I'm here, to learn about myself. I'm pretty ordinary, but I'm also extraordinary. Just like you."

"So when do I get to read this masterpiece?"

"Who knows."

"What do you mean?"

"I'm not sure. I guess we'll have to wait to see how the story ends."

"How did it begin?"

"It began with a whole lot of fear, but that feels pretty settled right now. I'm hoping that by tomorrow I'll have what I came for."

"And what is that?"

"A ring… at least that's what it is physically. In reality the ring just represents me. Everything in the world represents me… or you. That's the beauty of life."

"I'm not sure if I follow this," she said. "You started all this for a ring… the book and everything? Is it an ordinary ring?"

"Not exactly," I said to her. "It's an engagement ring."

"Oh, I see, so it's not ordinary at all. But I thought you said…"

"Yes, I know what I said… and it was the little sparklies in the ring that taught me that lesson. I came here to buy something extraordinary, but the greatest gift I'm leaving with is rather ordinary. I'm leaving with a greater appreciation of what I have, not what I want. I have everything I need to be happy. I thought that a ring, or a marriage would give that to me."

"But it won't?"

"It can't. Nothing can. But we can discover it where it is."

"And where is that?"

"Through our ordinary relationships," I said, "whether it be with my fiancée or you. I obviously don't know you as well as I know my fiancée… and I don't need to. But my appreciation of you can be the same, and I appreciate you just the way you are… in all the ordinary ways you live your life. Do you get it?"

"Not really… well, maybe a little. So, this is what you're writing about?"

"Yeah, I guess it is."

"Well, good luck," she said as she stood to leave. "Who knows, maybe it'll become a bestseller and the whole world will know how ordinary I am."

"Wouldn't we all be lucky."

"And you can go from mall to mall writing about all the ordinary record chicks you meet."

"I doubt it."

"Why not?"

"My retreat at the mall is nearly over."

"Retreat?"

"Yeah… it's a long story, but that's how I'm writing… never mind, it sounds crazy."

"Whatever. I just want editorial rights over my character."

"I promise I won't use your name."

"And steal my chance for fame? Better not. Just call me the Hip Record Chick."

"I already have."

Lesson 10

Love Conquers All

It was Friday afternoon, the final hours of my mall retreat. How much had I changed in five days, I wondered, as I walked down the long corridor looking at the stores that were by then so familiar? What spark was it that launched me toward this opening, so that even a mall could seem like home, the place where deep spiritual insights can be discovered and retained?

The fear I had felt when I first entered was nearly gone, replaced by a quiet feeling that had nothing at all to do with the bustling crowds and the anxious Christmas shoppers. The feeling was independent of these things, filled and refilled by a deep well that no one else could see but which I could certainly sense. Maybe it was more than a feeling — an even deeper experience that I could never hope to explain. Whatever it was I felt renewed, just as anyone should at the end of a retreat, and I knew I had achieved whatever it was I came to achieve.

I spent nearly an hour walking slowly through the mall, through all the department stores and shops. I looked at the people I passed and tried to see in them what I was feeling within myself. And in each eye I looked there was a spark of life that reflected my own joy, and the lessons seemed to come to a brilliant focus in my heart, radiating from there to everyone who had ever existed. Time felt as if it was collapsing around me and I could no longer tell where I ended and where the others began. Right there in the middle of the mall, of all places, I felt as if I was one with the whole universe, and everything seemed to make sense. It wasn't a ring I came to find, but myself through these others. Who would have known I could achieve so much in such a strange place?

Before I realized it I was standing in front of the shoe repair shop, and I saw my friend, the Shoe Man, staring at me silently. I walked closer and his smile never faded. He seemed to grow bigger and more important the closer I came, and I suddenly realized how essential his role had been in those five days while I searched for answers.

"Do you see now?" he asked when I walked up to the counter.

"Do I see? Yes, I think I do. I think I finally do."

"Tell me what it is you see, and we will both learn what a mall like this can give."

It was as if he was a different man, or I was seeing him in a way I hadn't before. The costume seemed to fall to the ground and he was no longer the Shoe Man I expected. His eyes were like radiant orbs that were not eyes at all, but whole universes. I know how strange that sounds, and I don't know if he had changed or I had. Perhaps I had been cast into a different level of perception and I was seeing for the first time what had always been present. I suddenly realized that my retreat was complete and it was nearly time to leave.

"I look around this place where a week before I saw nothing but confusion," I said, "but now everything is different. Take you for example... you seem like a different person, like you're a Zen Master or something." He didn't say a word, just maintained the eye lock that told me I had hit the mark.

"Is that the truth? You're really a master masquerading as a shoe repairman? Why didn't I see this before? It's so obvious."

"You still haven't told me what you've learned," he said.

"You mean what I'm learning... this very moment. Nothing is the way it seems, is it? I came here with all this fear, but I've discovered something far more important than I thought possible. The truth is everywhere, in everyone, especially in the places and people where we don't want it to be. I decided to do a retreat at the mall because I didn't like malls. Now here I am seeing God everywhere I look."

"And has the mall changed, or have you?" he asked.

"The mall hasn't changed, that's obvious. Many of the same people are still here, like you, but I'm seeing them through new eyes. You haven't changed, have you? You're still repairing shoes like you were five days ago, smiling at everyone whose eyes meet yours and throwing out little bits of wisdom to anyone who will listen. Even I haven't changed, but the way I'm looking at everything has. I'm seeing what has always been there, but which I was blind to before."

"What was it you were blind to before?" he asked as he picked up a shoe and rubbed it with a cloth.

"I was blind to love, I guess. I was saying that there are some places, like this mall, where love is harder to find. But it isn't. It's always been here. I just had to open my eyes and see it. It doesn't even matter how love appears, because it will never be the same. But that's the real lesson — that love is always present, even when it doesn't seem to be."

"And so…"

"And so what?" I asked.

"What now? Where do you go from here?"

I had to stop and think about that one. Was it time to leave? Was that what he was asking? And if it was, where would I go? Maybe it didn't really matter where I went, but that I took this lesson and applied it everywhere, whether I was in a mall or sitting alone in my own room. Love, after all, transcends those definitions and is natural in every situation. If I want love more than everything else, then I'll find it wherever I go.

"Nowhere," I said to him. "I won't go anywhere at all because this was the only real lesson I came to learn. Love is the only goal, and we achieve that goal by diving into our fear and letting it be transformed by love. So I don't need to go anywhere. Of course I'll leave this mall and travel wherever I need to travel, but that doesn't matter. My heart will stay exactly where it is now."

"So love is the only answer," he said. "You've spent a week shining your soul like I've shined this shoe, and now you can see so much clearer."

"Exactly. I was just a little dull when I came in here. But that's changed now, thanks to you and everyone else I met."

"I did nothing. I'm just an ordinary shoe repair man."

"Yes you are, and that's all you need to be. That's why the lesson worked so well."

There was one final thing to accomplish before my retreat would reach its end. I had to leave with the engagement ring, and feel perfect joy at its reception; otherwise the primary objective would not have been reached. It was the reason I began this odyssey, and to leave prematurely would be an omen I could not bear. All the lessons and insights hinged upon this, for I would need one final demonstration to show I had truly conquered my fear.

I went up the escalator and stood a few feet away from Raffi Jewelers. My breath was heavy and I could feel my heart beating very fast. It was the final episode, the culmination of five days of reflection and self-observation. I had learned so much, but the ring was like a final prize, the crown of victory that would permeate every lesson.

I stepped into the store.

"Hello there," Peter said when he saw me. "I have very good news for you."

It was a good beginning. If he didn't have the ring he would have told me right away. The fact that he was walking toward me with a smile meant my timing was perfect.

"You have the ring? It's finished?" I asked.

"Yes, it's finished, but there's something else you need to know."

This was not expected. I didn't need anything else to finalize my adventure. What other objective could there be but that? What added bonus had I earned from five days of serious introspection?

"First of all," he continued, "the ring is beautiful. Your fiancée is going to love it. But we had a little problem when we were trying to set the diamonds."

"A problem?"

"Yes. Siri Rishi's fingers are very small and it seems I underestimated how many diamonds were needed. You ordered an eternity band with the diamonds going all the way around. When we were setting them we realized that there was a gap, and at first we didn't know what to do."

"A gap?"

"Yes, a gap. There were two options. One was to simply keep the gap. It wouldn't have been a real problem since it would be on the backside. No one would ever see it."

"A gap?" I said again.

"The other option was the one we chose. I thought you would like it better. We threw in an extra diamond for free. That completed the circle and now it is perfect."

"An extra diamond. That's what your choice was? You gave me an extra diamond?"

"Is there a problem with that?"

"You have no idea what this means," I said, becoming very emotional. "It's a sign, a final nod that says my lessons are complete. It means I learned everything I came here to learn."

"I don't think I understand."

"It's too hard to explain, but it's perfect. I came here to buy a ring but in the end I received so much more. And now you throw in an extra diamond. You have no idea what this means to me."

Peter looked at me strangely, as if he wasn't sure he had made the right choice after all. Then he unlocked the cabinet, took out a small box and opened it.

"Here it is," he said as he showed me the ring. "Isn't it beautiful?"

I took the ring in my hand and watched the light reflect off the diamonds. It was truly beautiful, like a band of pure radiance. What other sign did I need to end my time at the mall? What finale would equal this one, this last moment when all the lessons and insights came together like the diamonds on the ring I held? I looked up at Peter and smiled.

"Yes... it was worth the wait," I said to him. "You did a wonderful job, Peter."

"It was my brother who made the ring. We're a team. But it makes it all worthwhile when I see the look on your face. Like I said before, 'this isn't really about a ring, or jewelry at all. It's about love'. Love conquers everything because like these diamonds, it reflects the light and illumines all the dark places we hold. When you give this to Siri Rishi think about that. Whenever you doubt love, think about this ring and what it represents. Then you'll remember to do the same thing — reflect love. Isn't that the real lesson? Isn't that the only reason we're really here?"

"I think you're right on," I said.

"What other reason could there be?"

Acknowledgments

I would like to dedicate this book to Siri Rishi who has taught me how to live love, not just talk about it. I would also like to thank everyone who helped me put these ideas on paper — Sharon Williams, Stephanie Kern, Joanna Karl, Drayton Stevenson, Shirley Harvank, Gloria Kovcevich and Debbye Caughenour.

For information about James Twyman's work
and schedule of events, please consult
www.emissaryoflight.com

James F Twyman's works published by Findhorn Press

  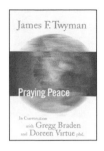 

Portrait of the Master

"This story, based on the life of St. Francis, will stir your soul, and could become an instant classic."
—Neale Donald Walsch, author of *Conversations with God*

Hard Cover   ISBN 1-899171-43-6

The Secret of the Beloved Disciple

Much of what you will read in this book may not make sense if you read it with your mind. But open your heart and it will speak directly to your soul, and you will understand some of the eternal secrets and mysteries of our purpose and destiny on this planet.

Paperback   ISBN 1-899171-08-8

Praying Peace

James F Twyman in conversation with Gregg Braden and Doreen Virtue, PhD

Whatever we focus our mind on grows. When we pray "for" peace, we focus on the lack of peace. If our intention is to be peace, then our prayers will reflect that and become peace, thus allowing more peace and harmony to be perceived by all.

Paperback   ISBN 1-899171-48-7

The Praying Peace Cards *(October 2001)*

These cards are a tool for creating harmony in your life by using portions of the peace prayers from all the major religions of the world. Forty-nine cards contain a short excerpt from a traditional prayer of peace, along with three "Flow Cards", Surrender, Trust and Gratitude.

Set of 52 cards   ISBN 1-899171-09-6

FINDHORN Press

Findhorn Press is the publishing business of the Findhorn Community which has grown around the Findhorn Foundation in northern Scotland.

For further information about the Findhorn Foundation and the Findhorn Community, please contact:

Findhorn Foundation
The Visitors Centre
The Park, Findhorn IV36 3TY, Scotland, UK
tel 01309 690311• fax 01309 691301
email reception@findhorn.org
www.findhorn.org

For a complete Findhorn Press catalogue, please contact:

Findhorn Press

The Park, Findhorn,
Forres IV36 3TY
Scotland, UK
Tel 01309 690582
freephone 0800-389-9395
Fax 01309 690036

P. O. Box 13939
Tallahassee
Florida 32317-3939, USA
Tel (850) 893 2920
toll-free 1-877-390-4425
Fax (850) 893 3442

e-mail info@findhornpress.com
www.findhornpress.com